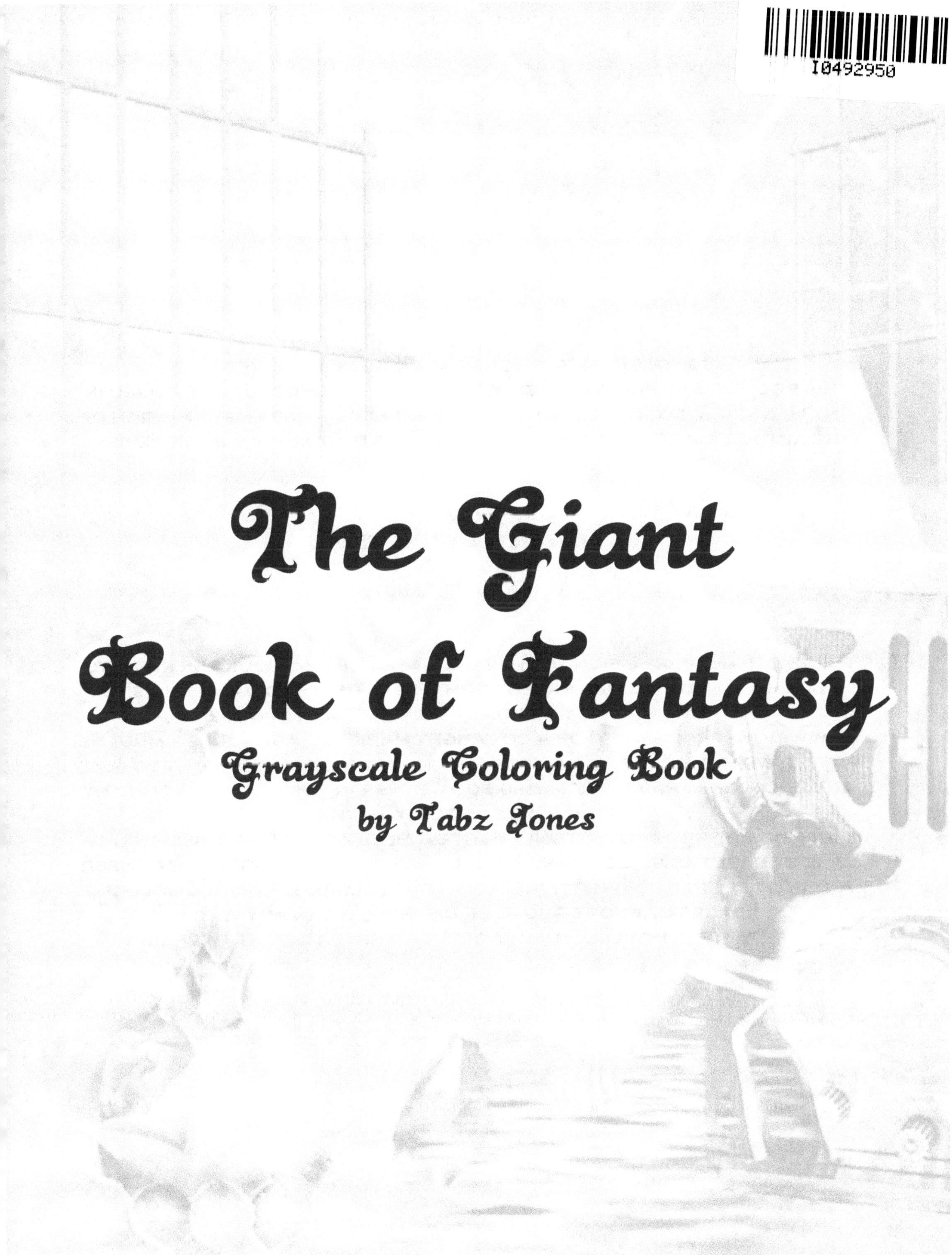

The Giant Book of Fantasy

Grayscale Coloring Book

by Tabz Jones

TABZ JONES
410 CRESTVIEW ACRES CIRCLE
ALMA, AR 72921
GOTHIC_TOGGS@YAHOO.COM

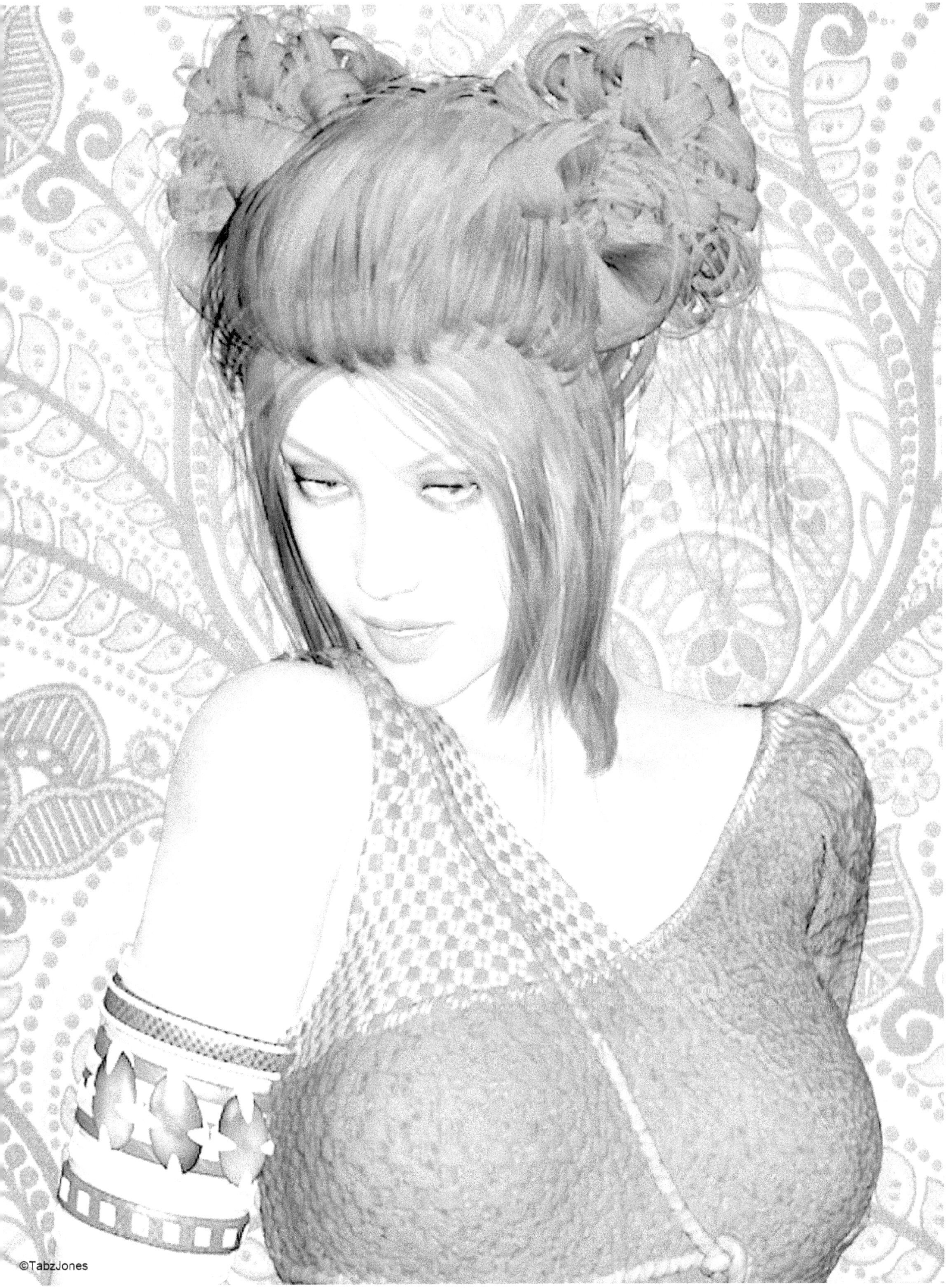

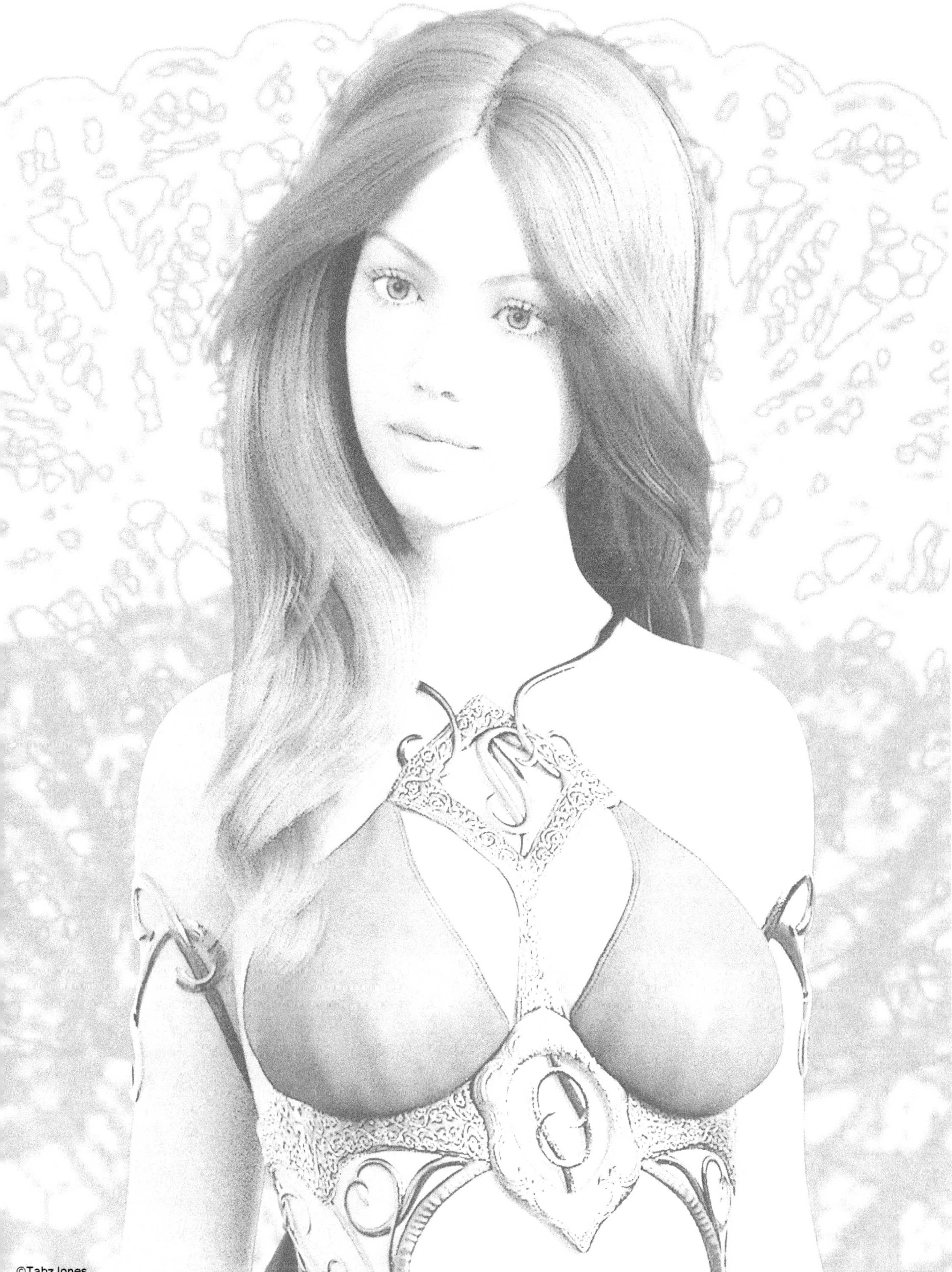

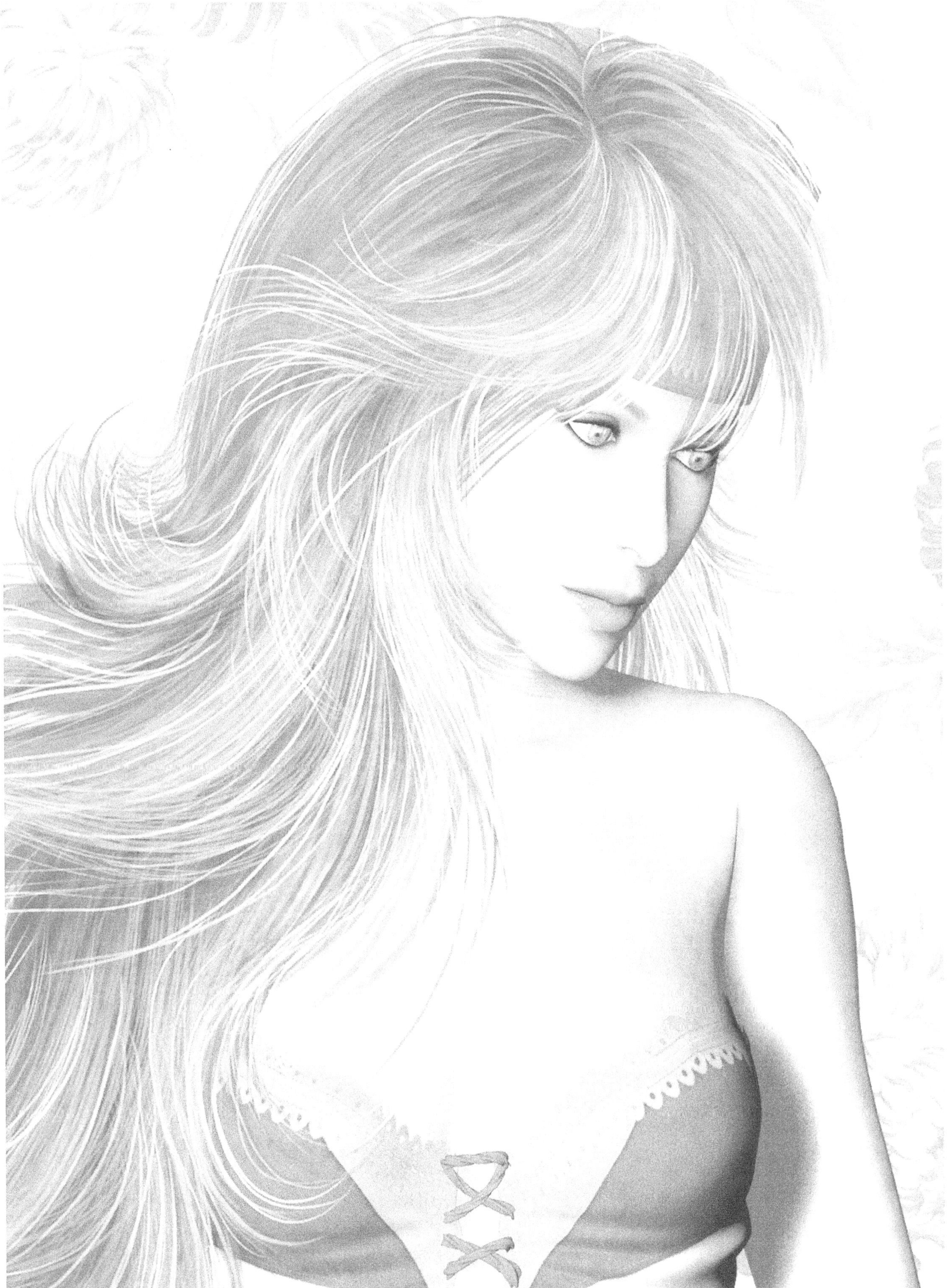
©TabzJones

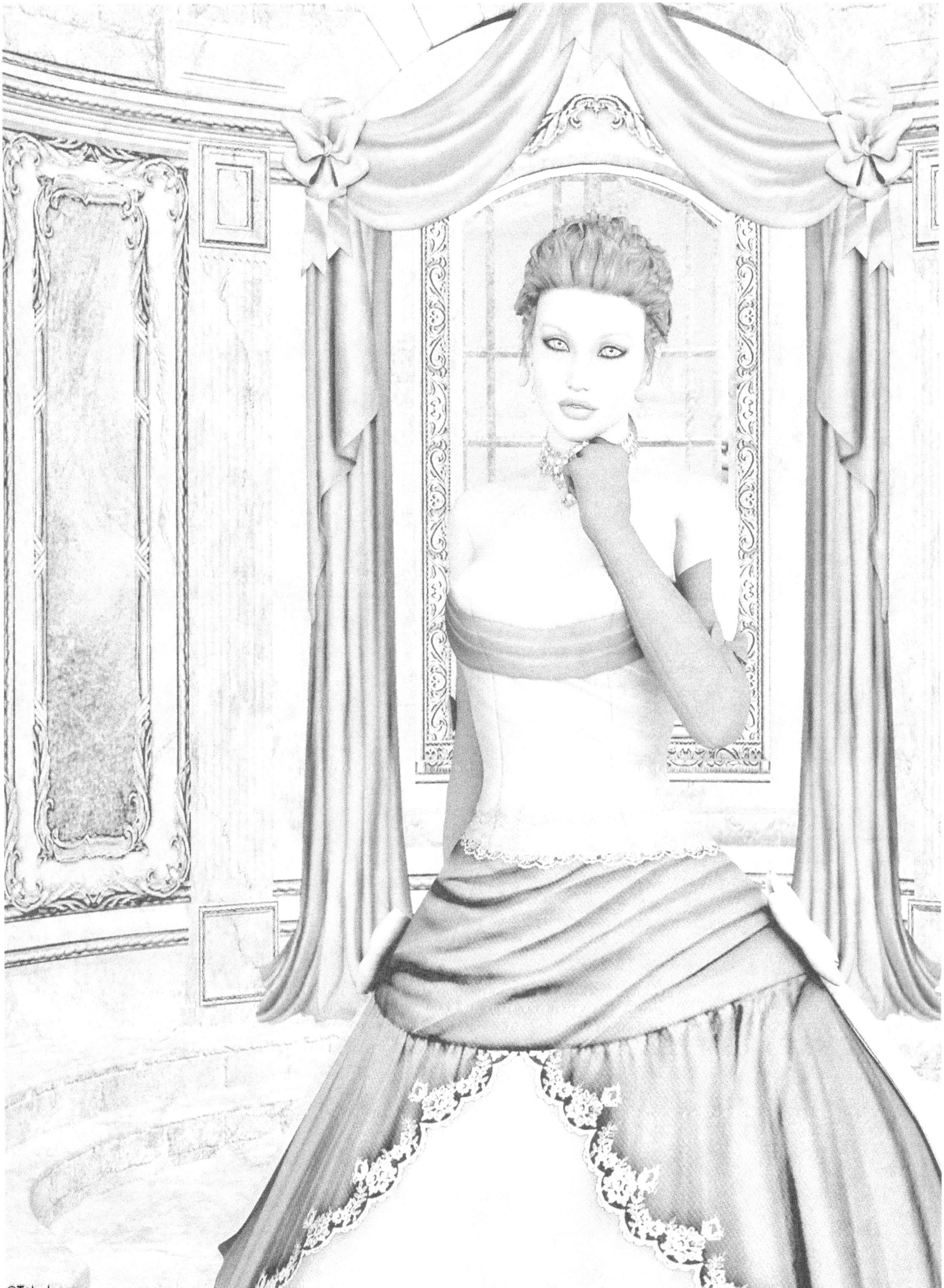

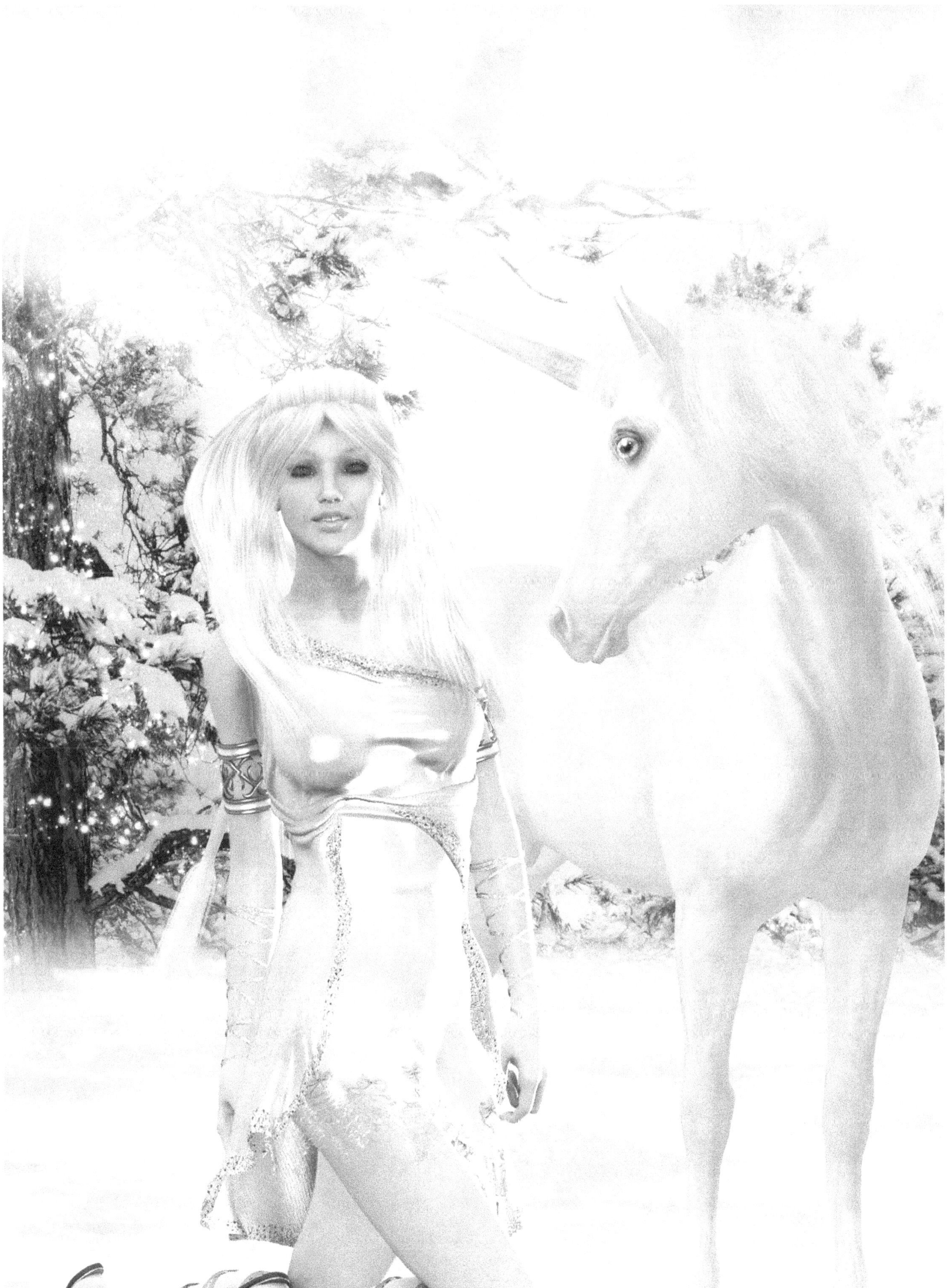

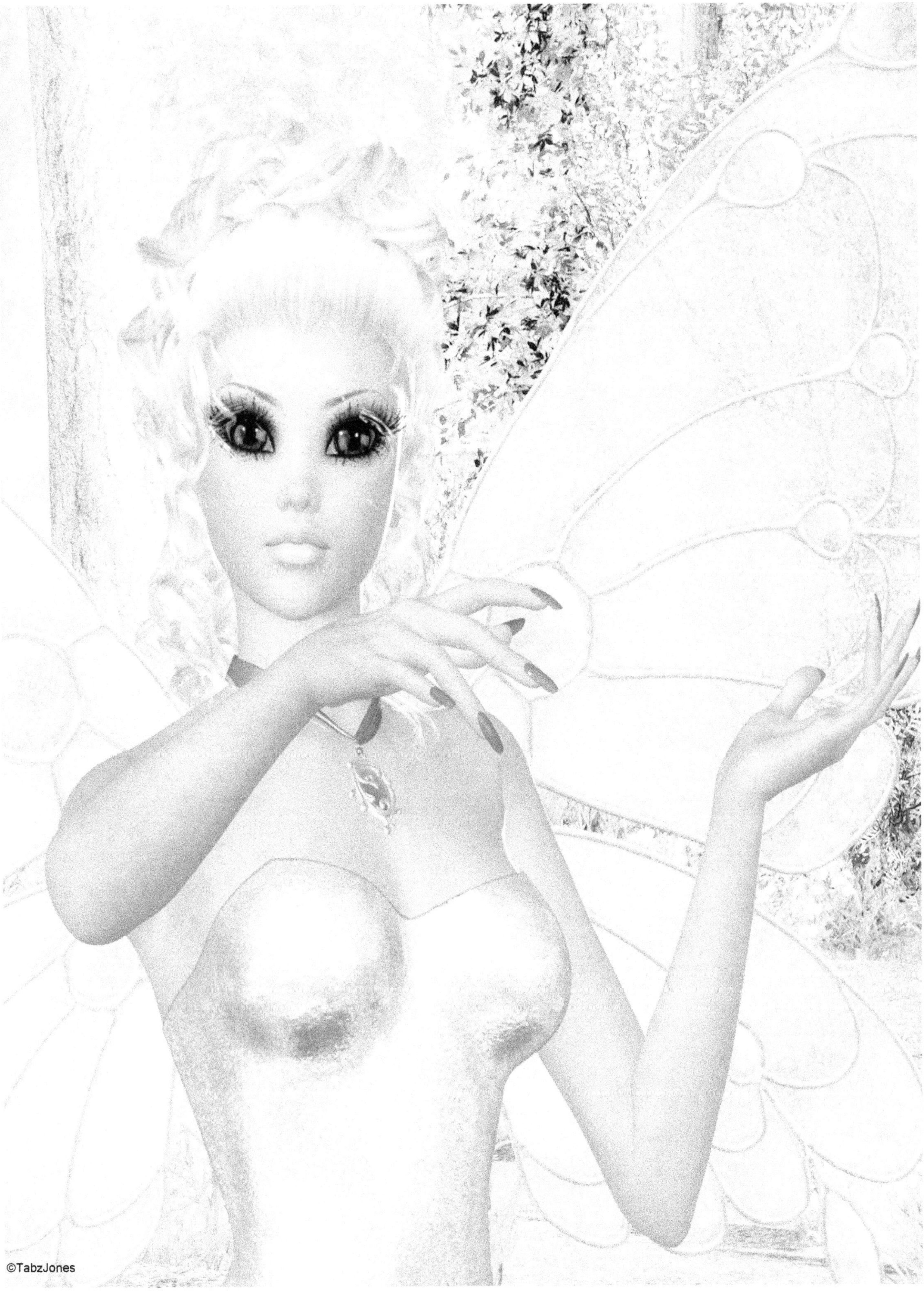

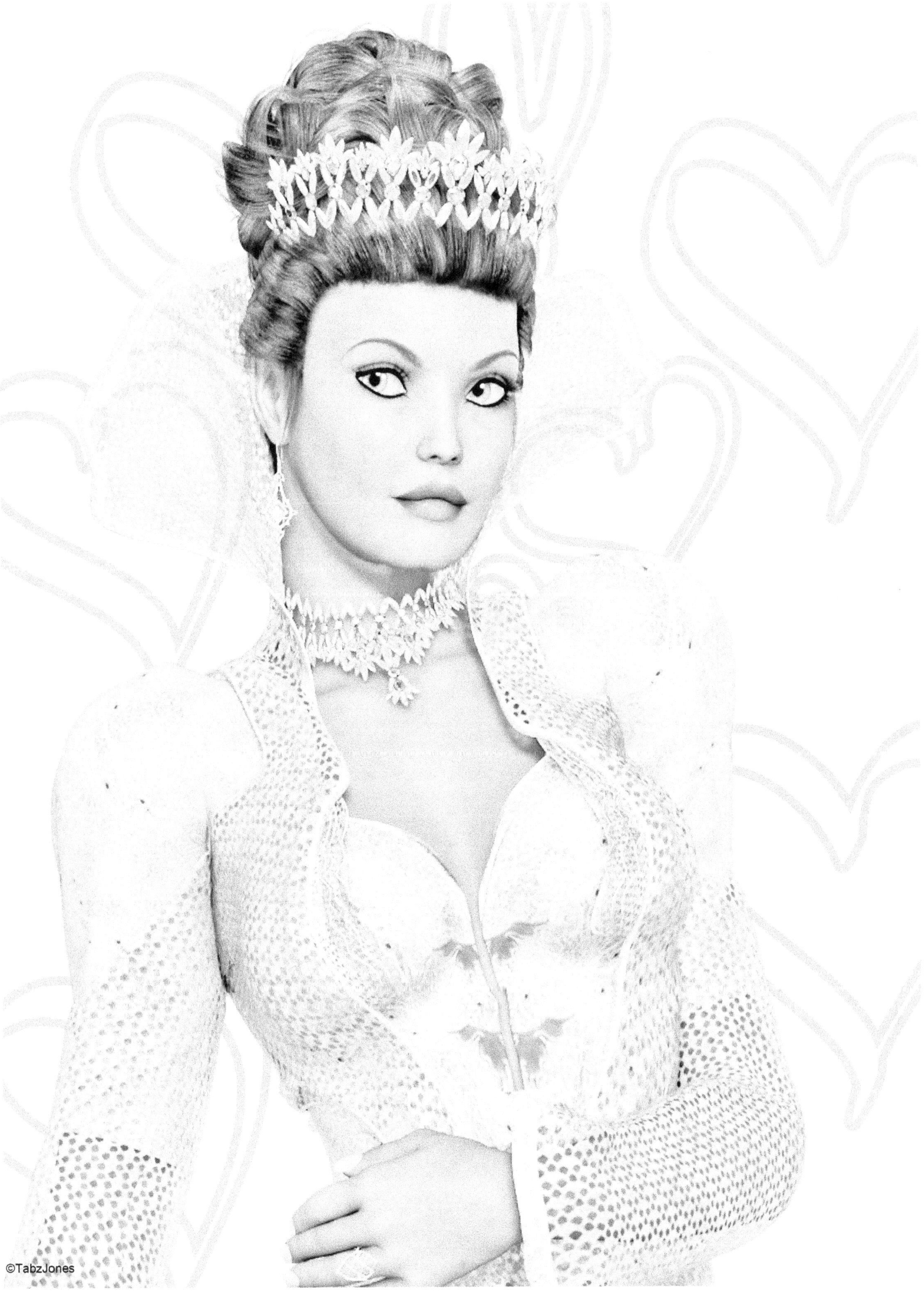

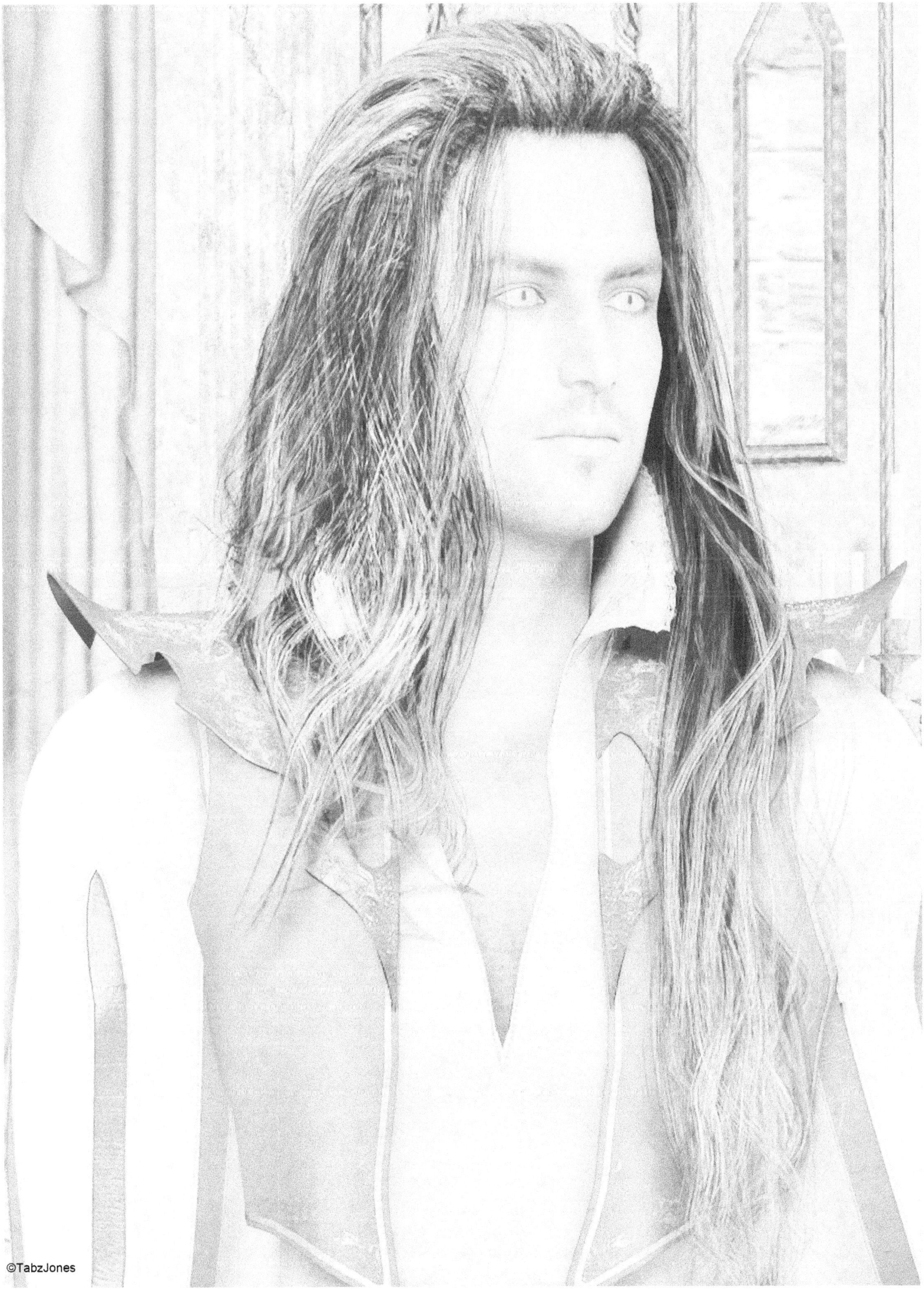

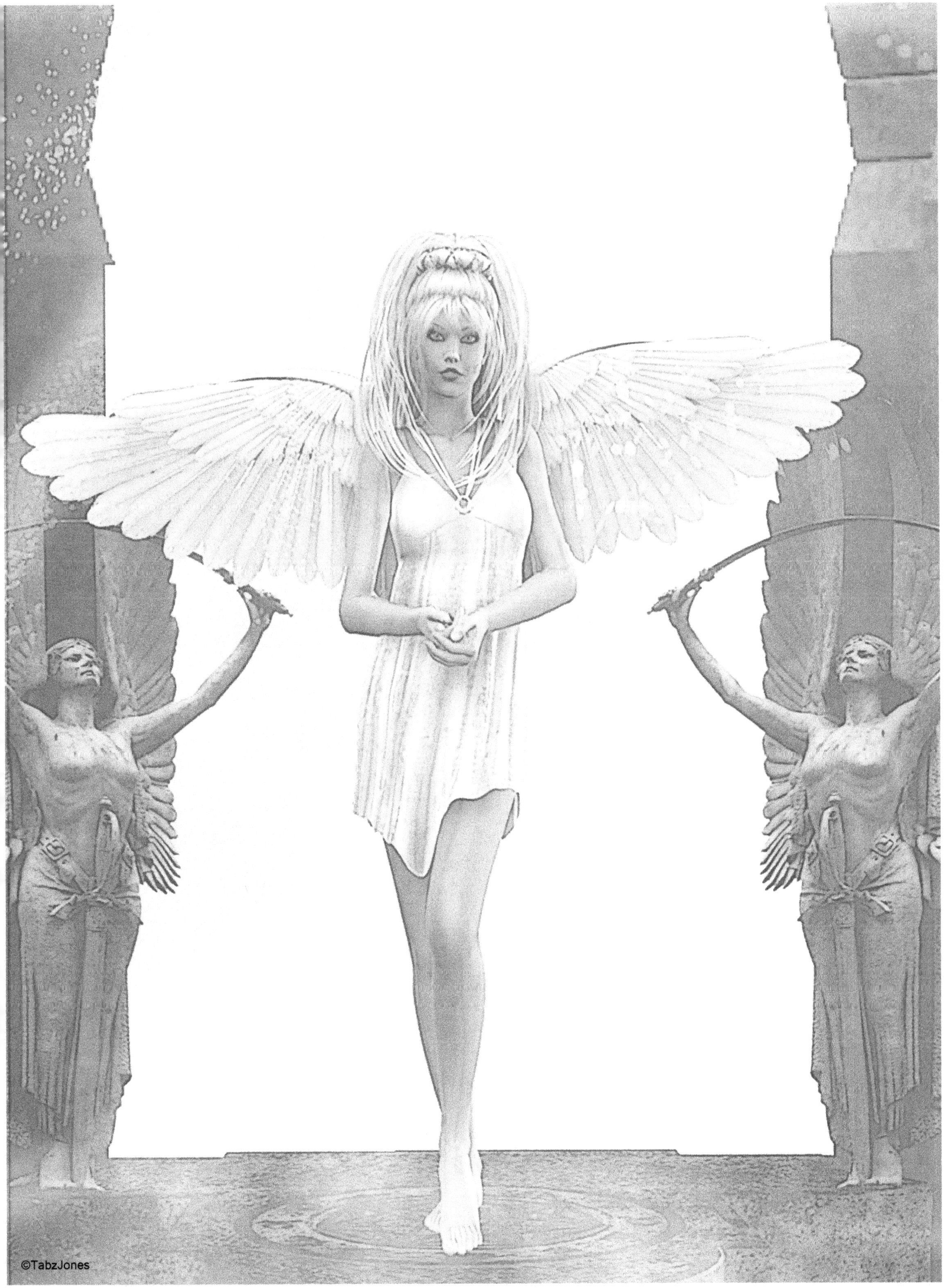

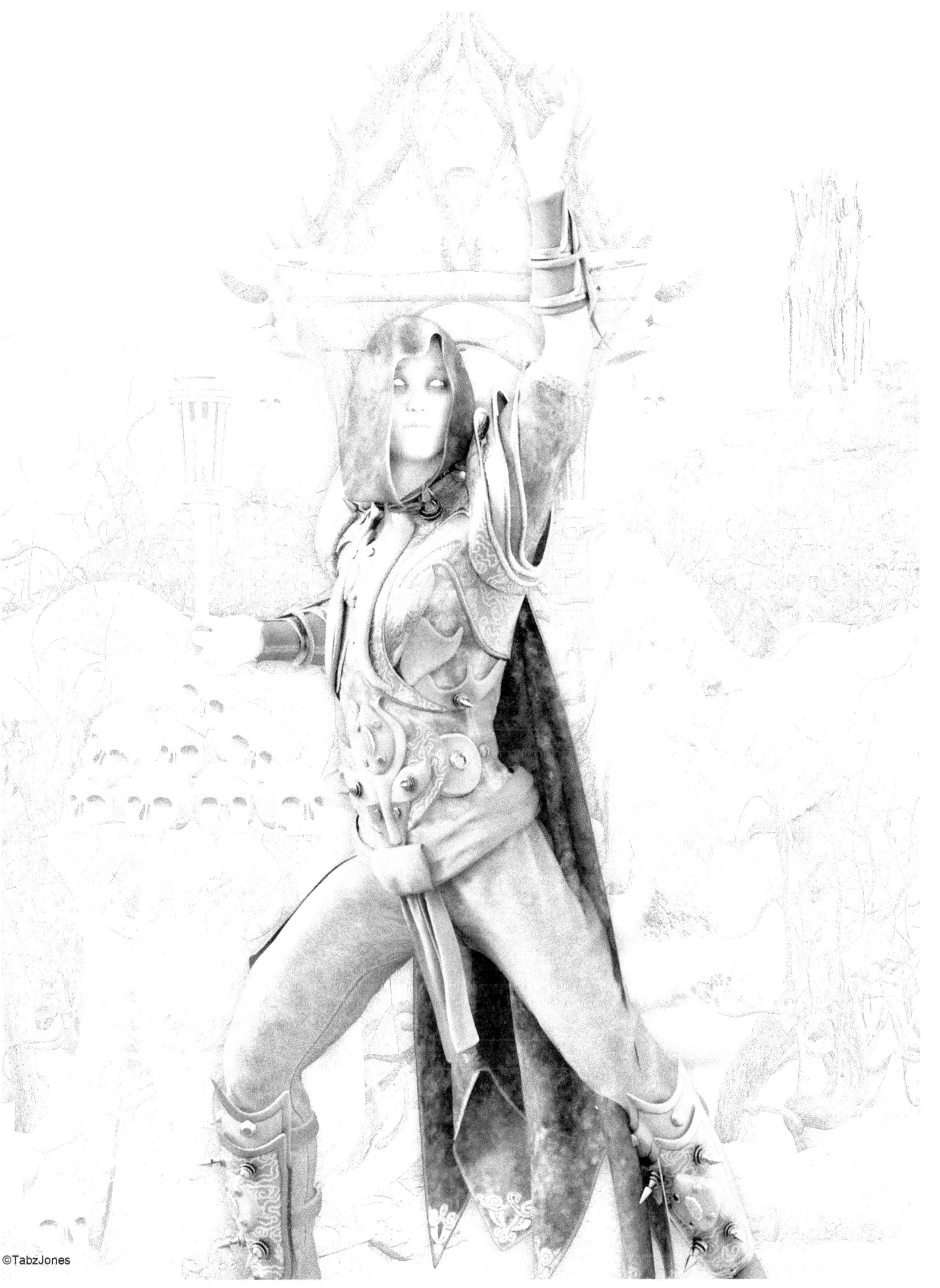

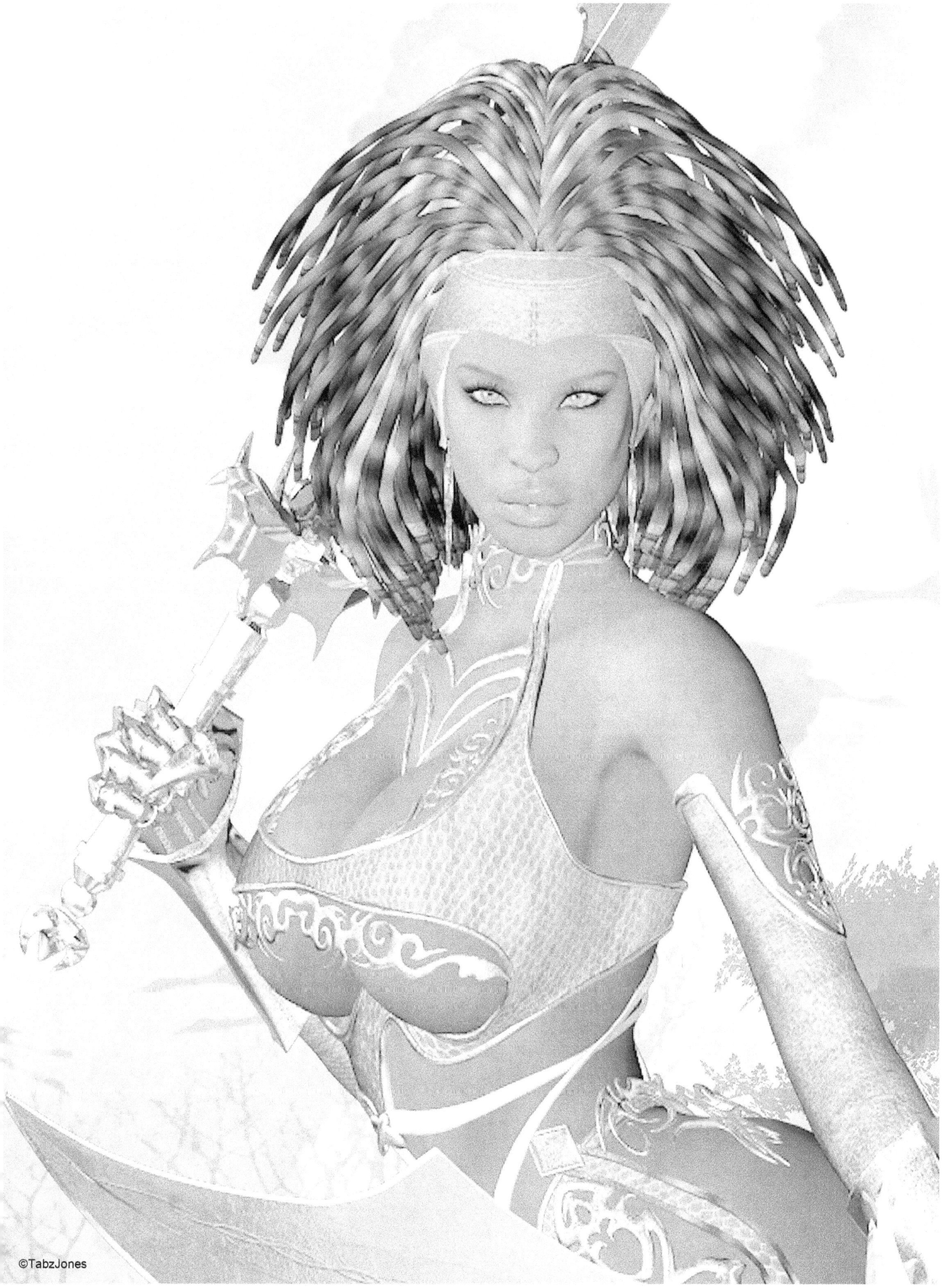

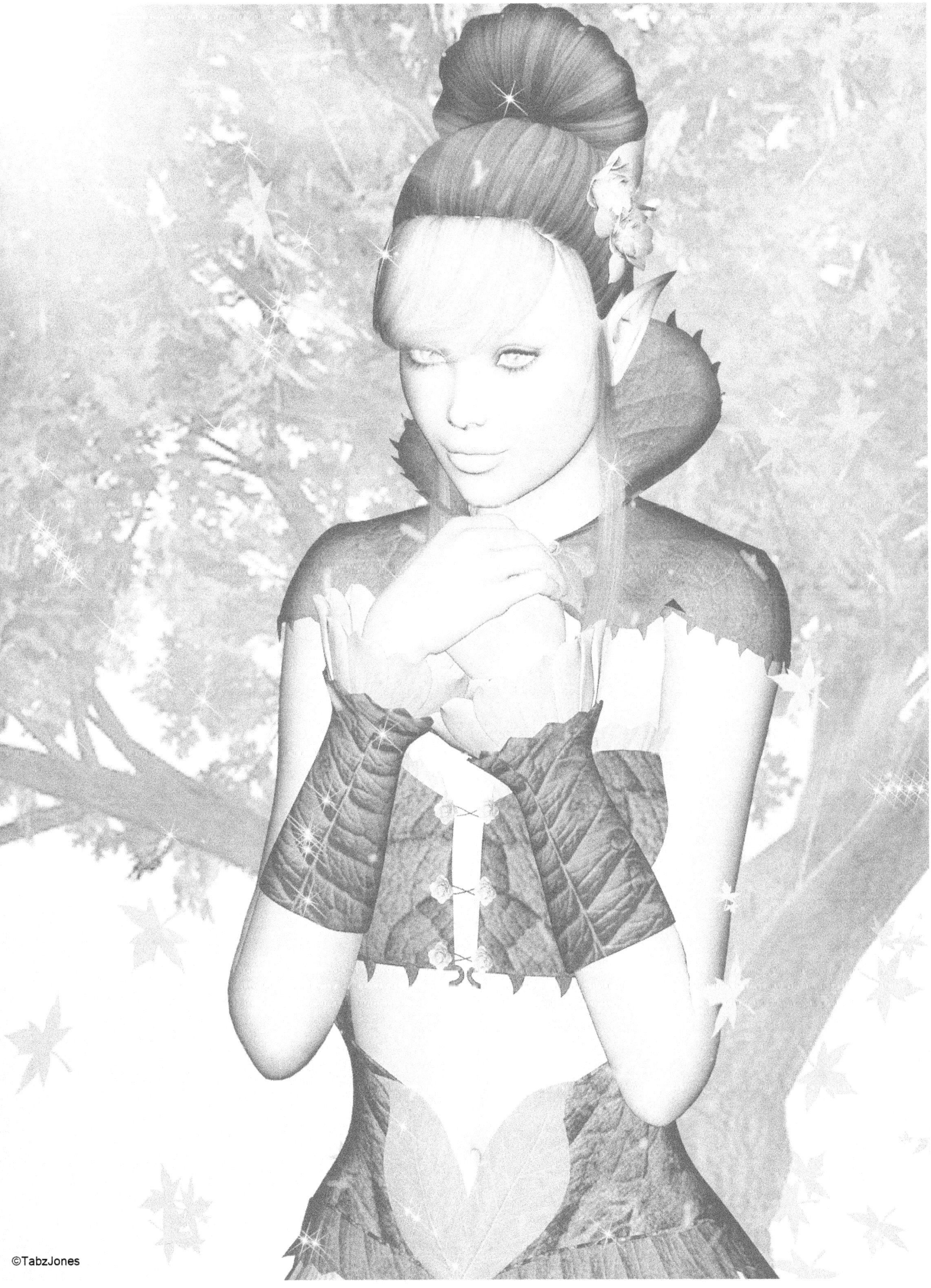

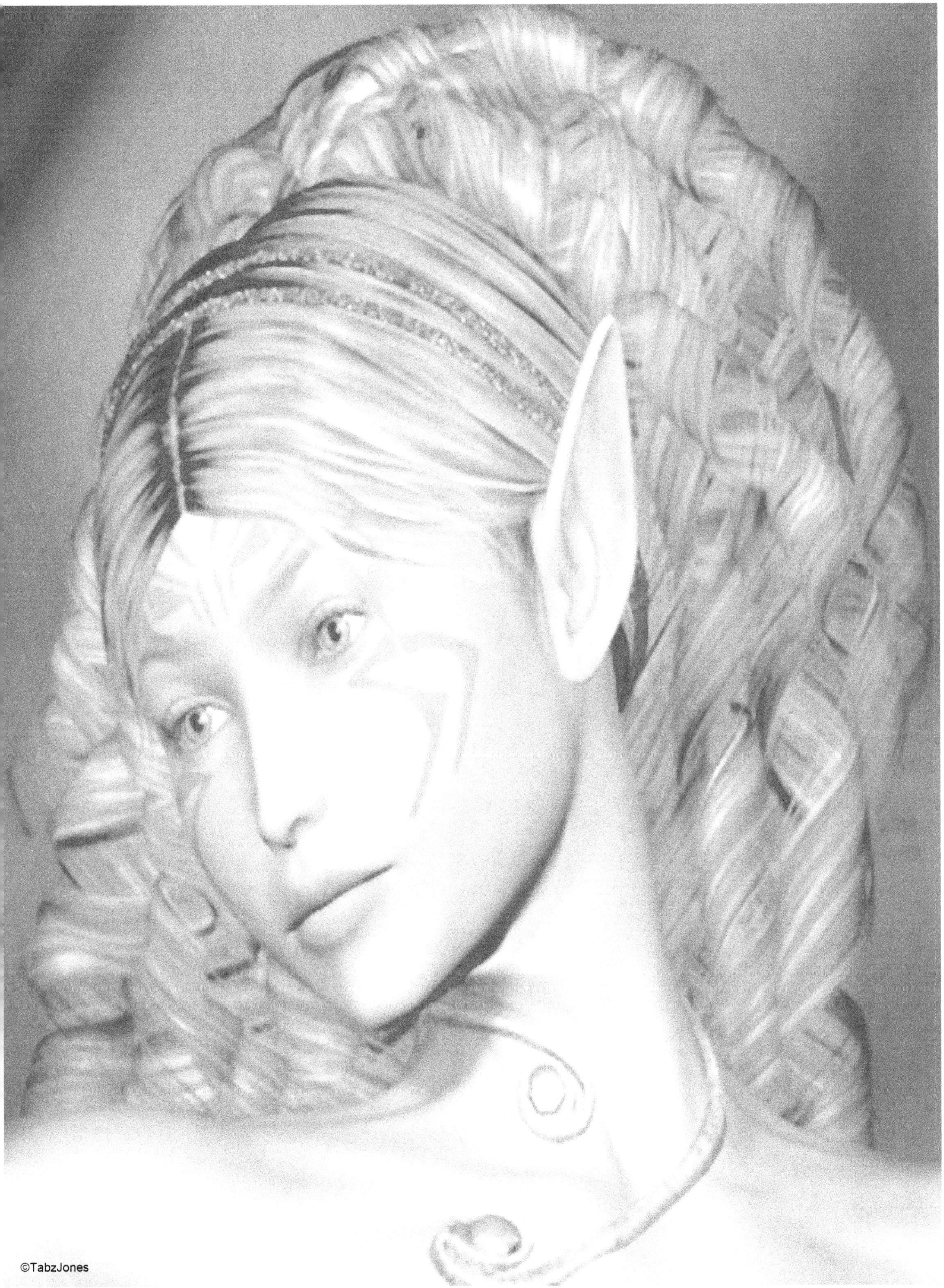

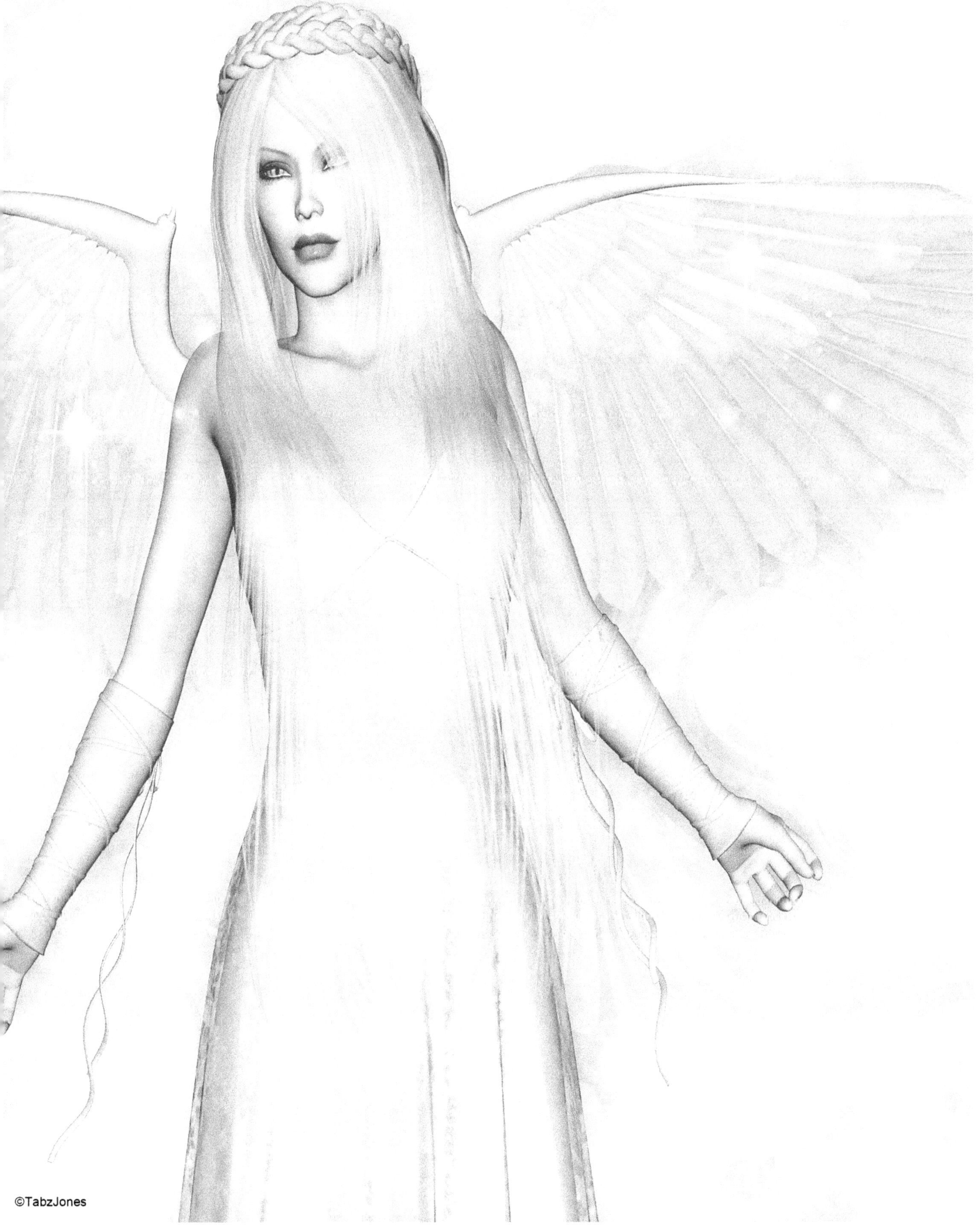

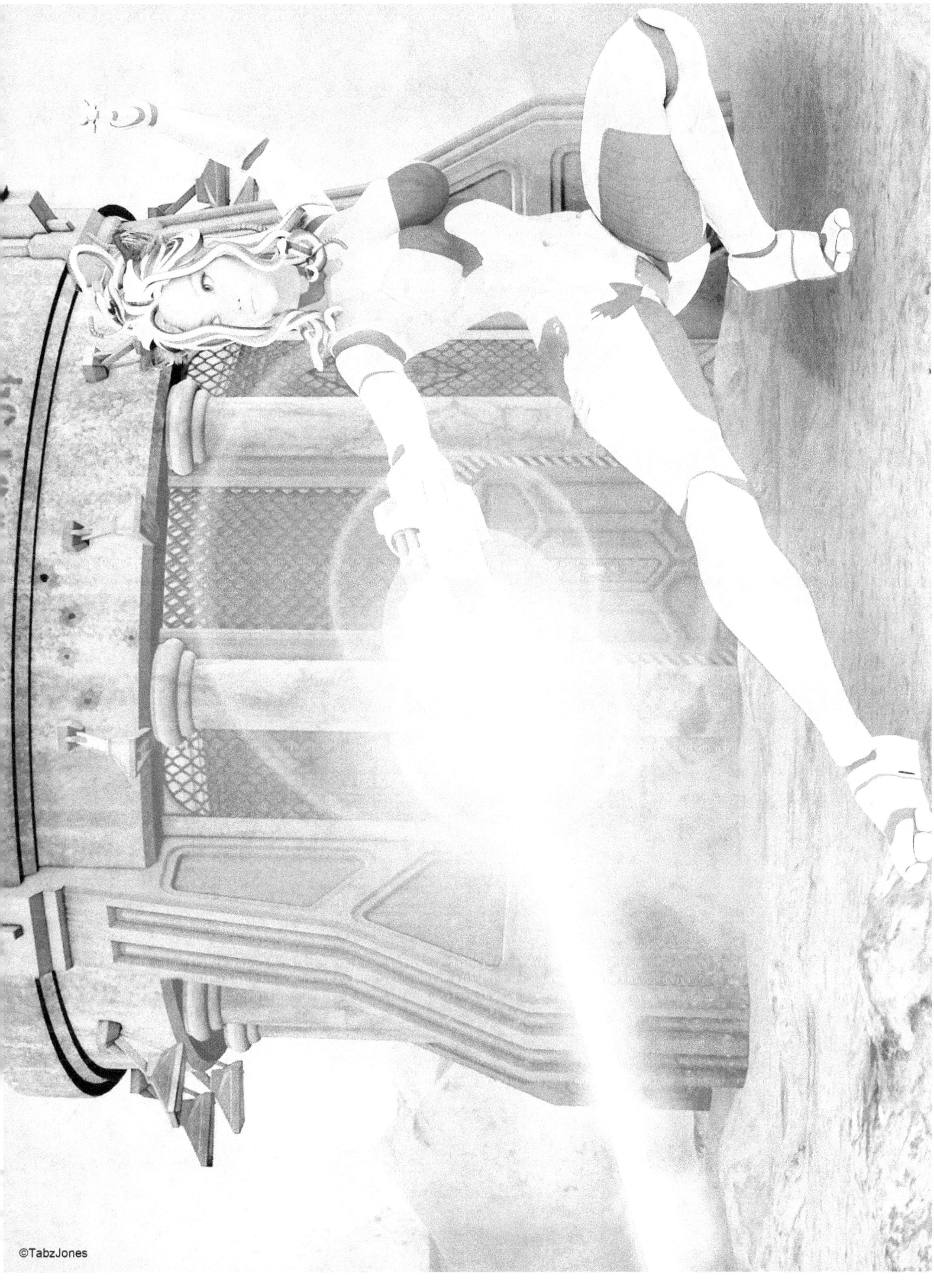

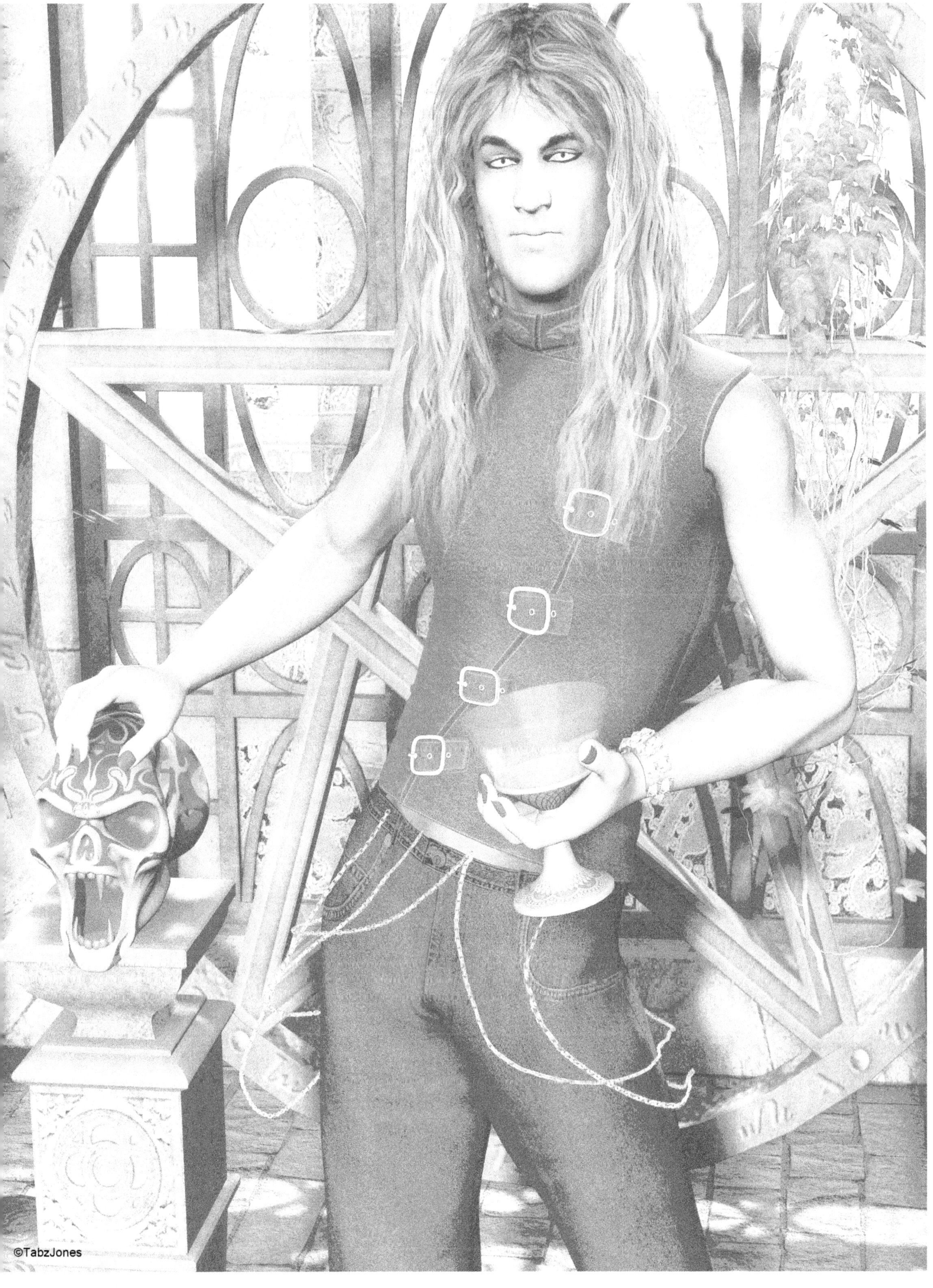

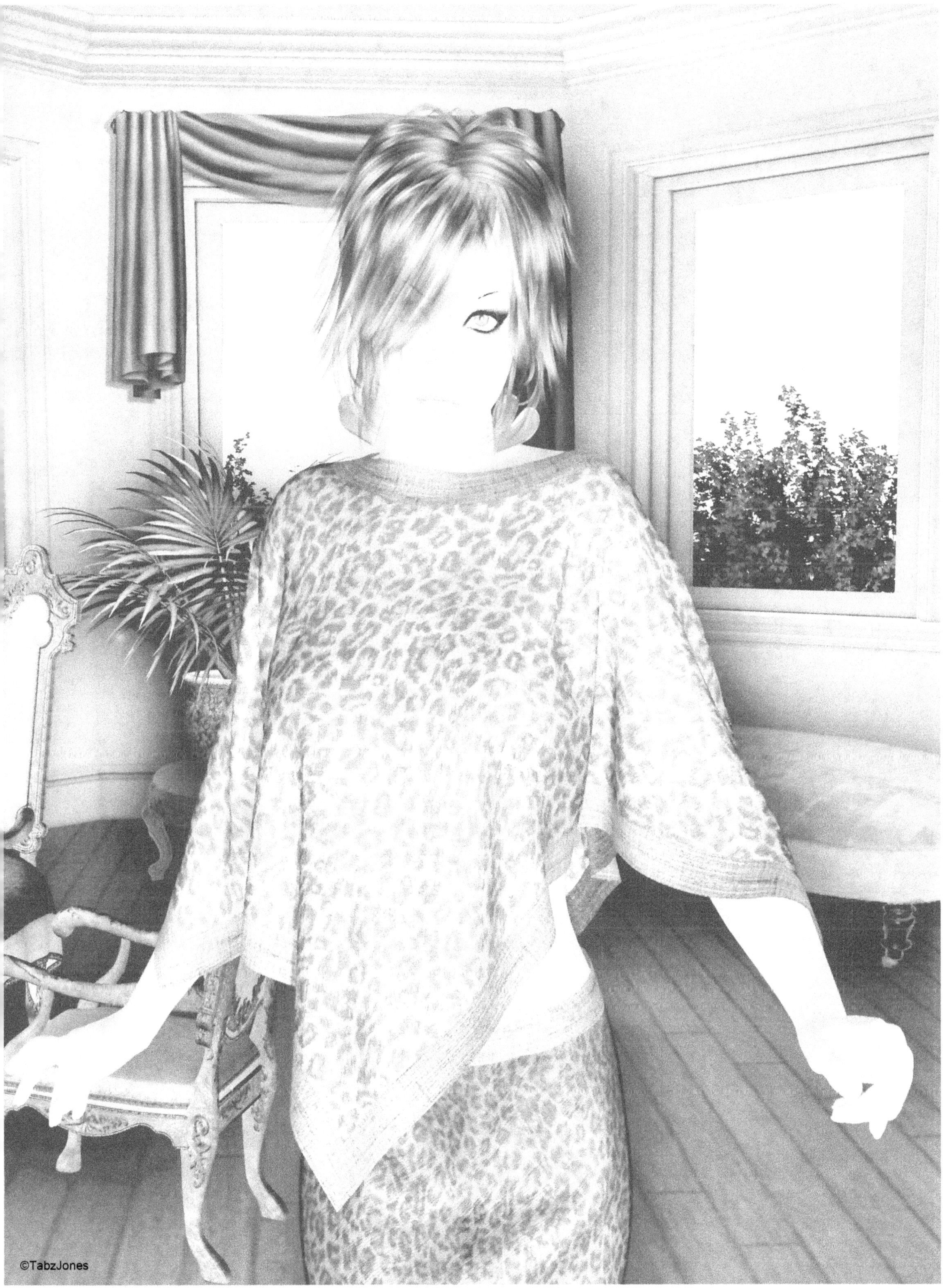

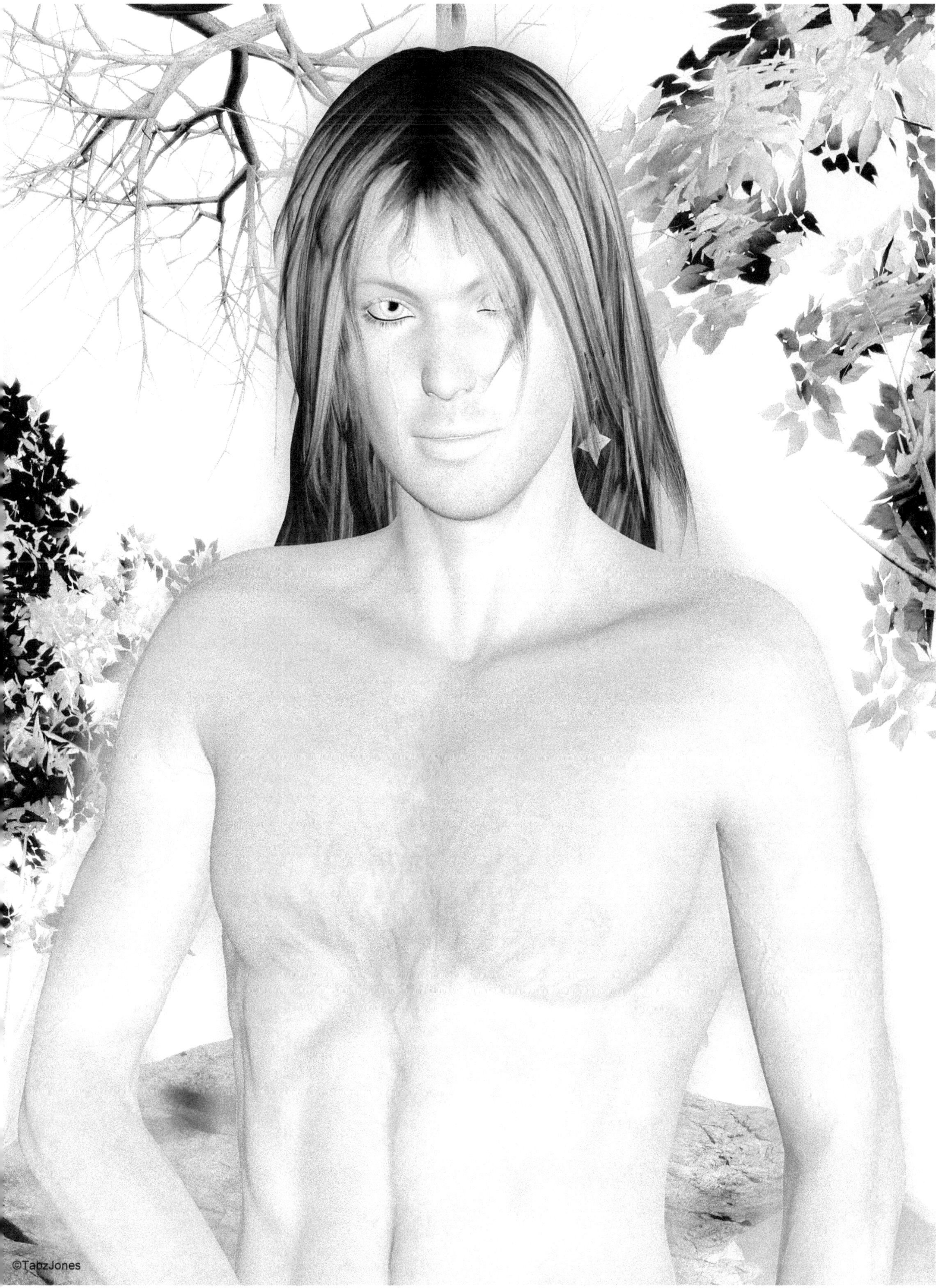
©TabzJones

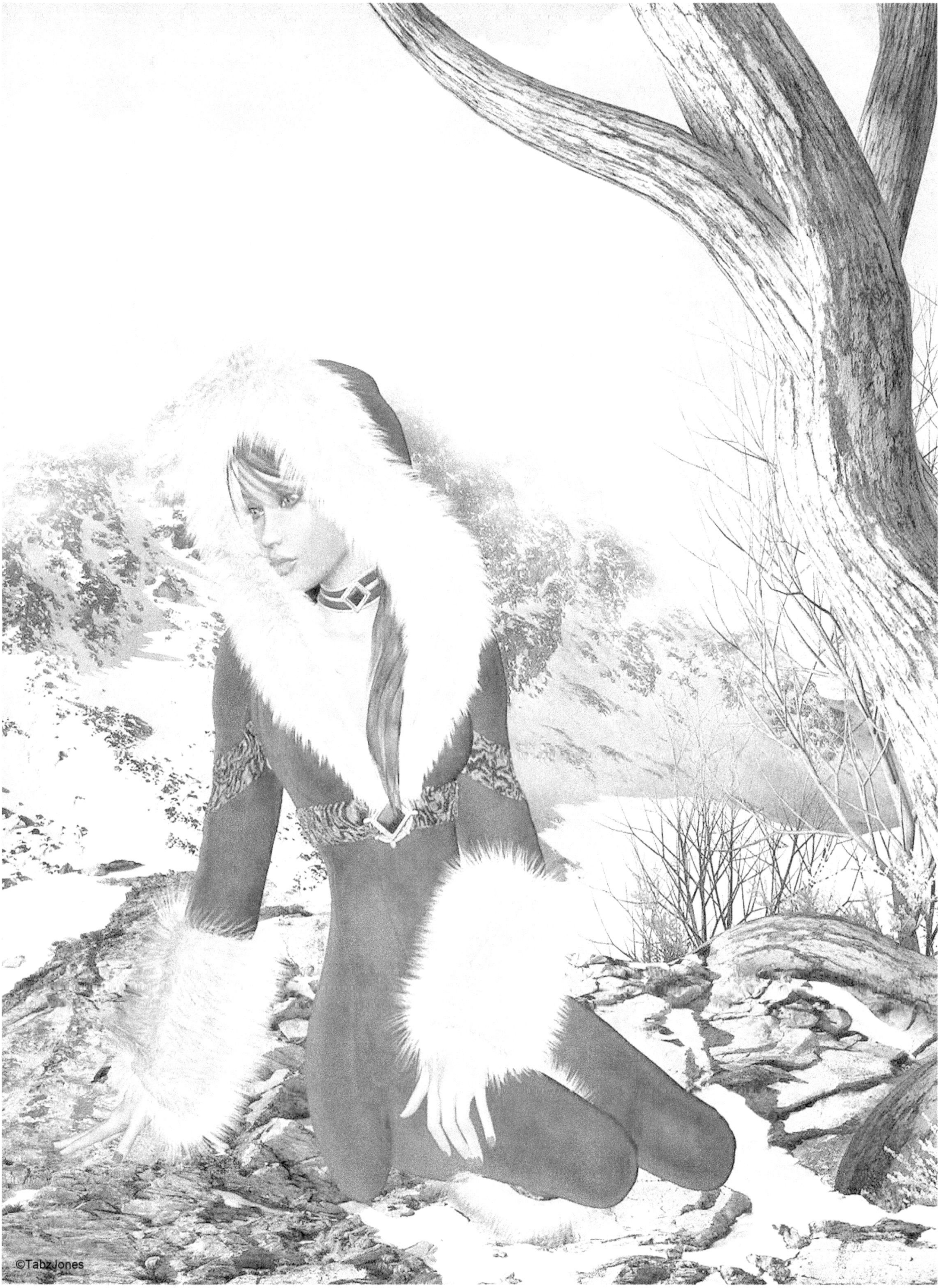
©TabzJones

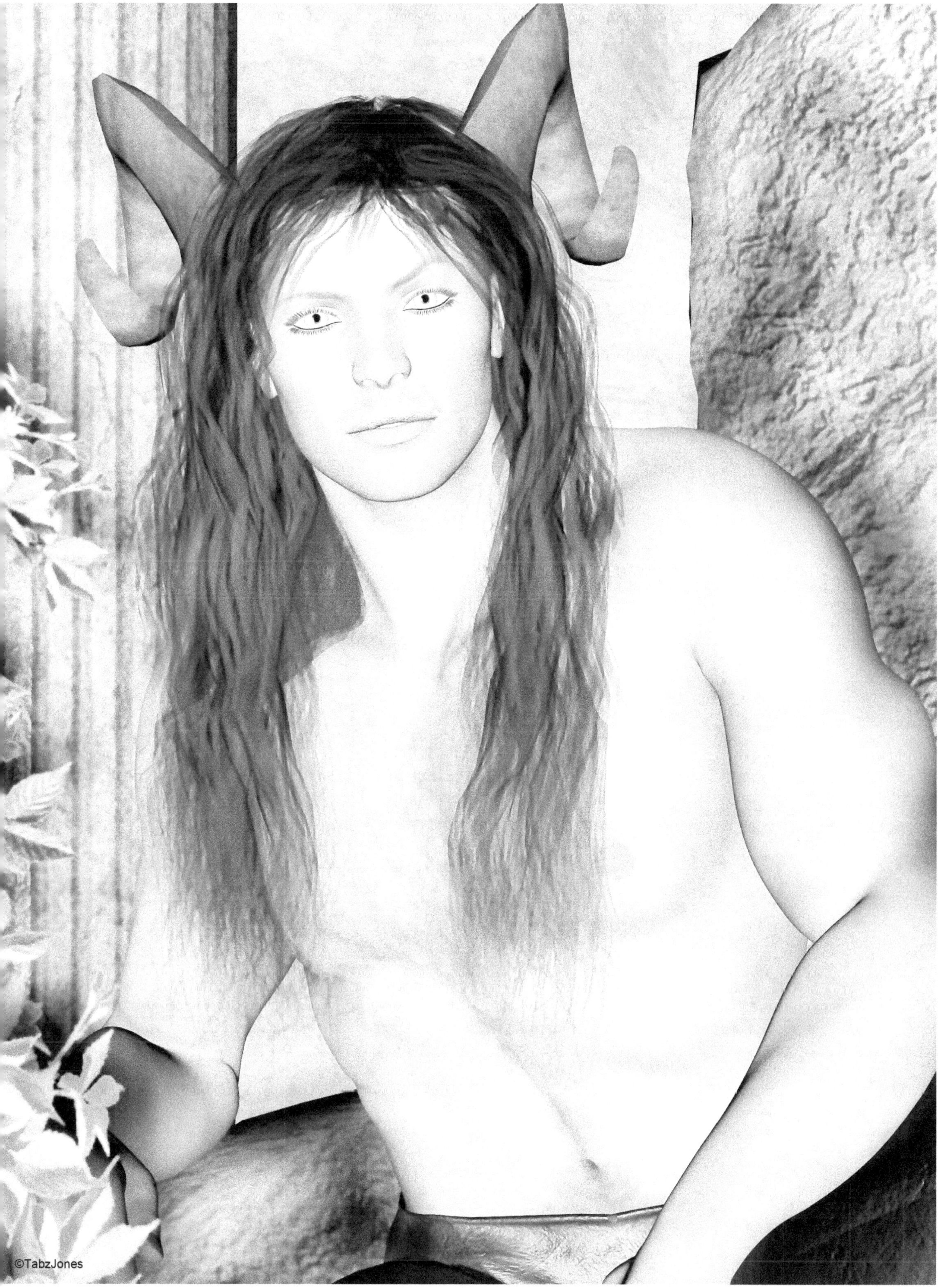
©TabzJones

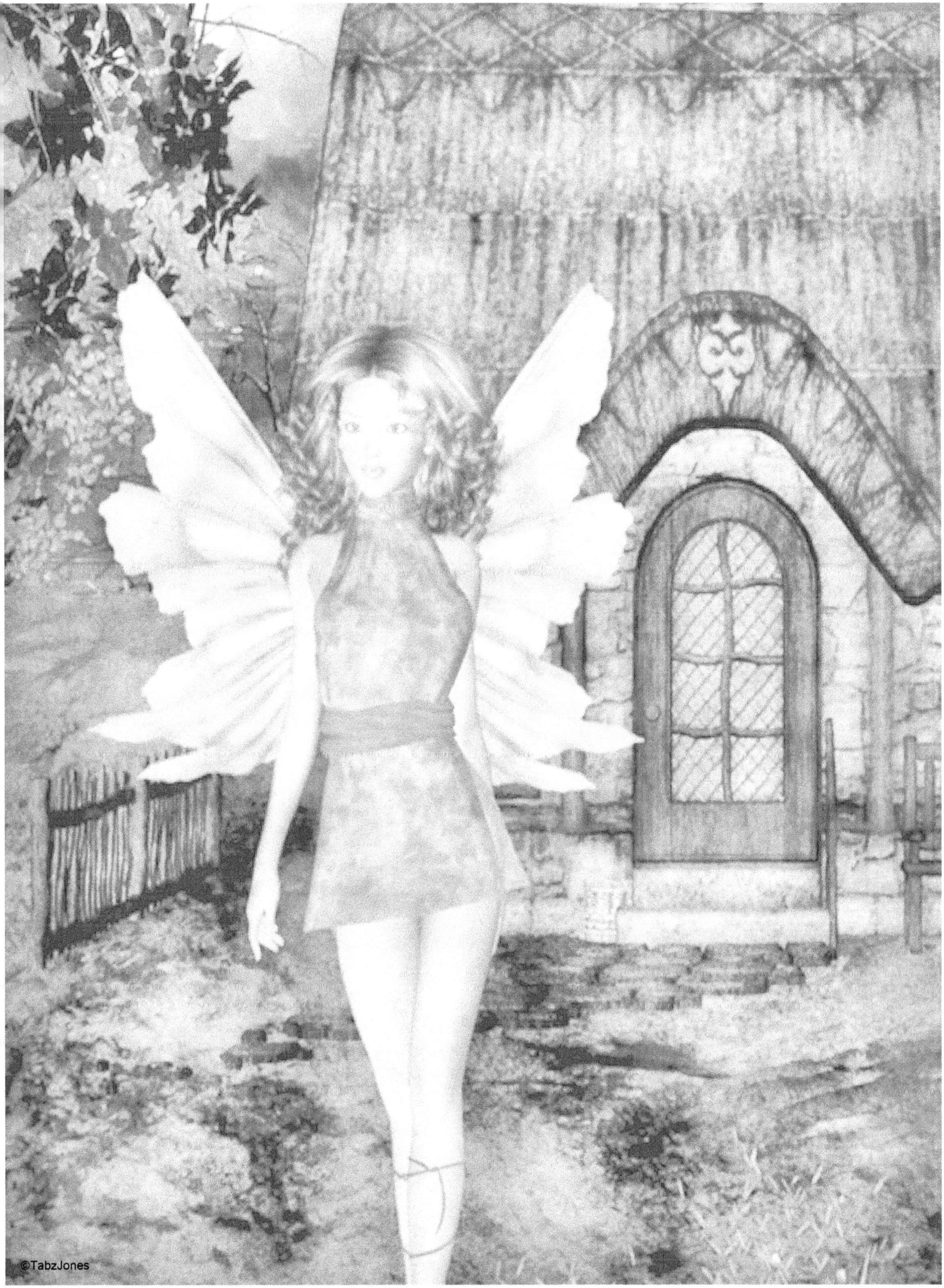
©TabzJones

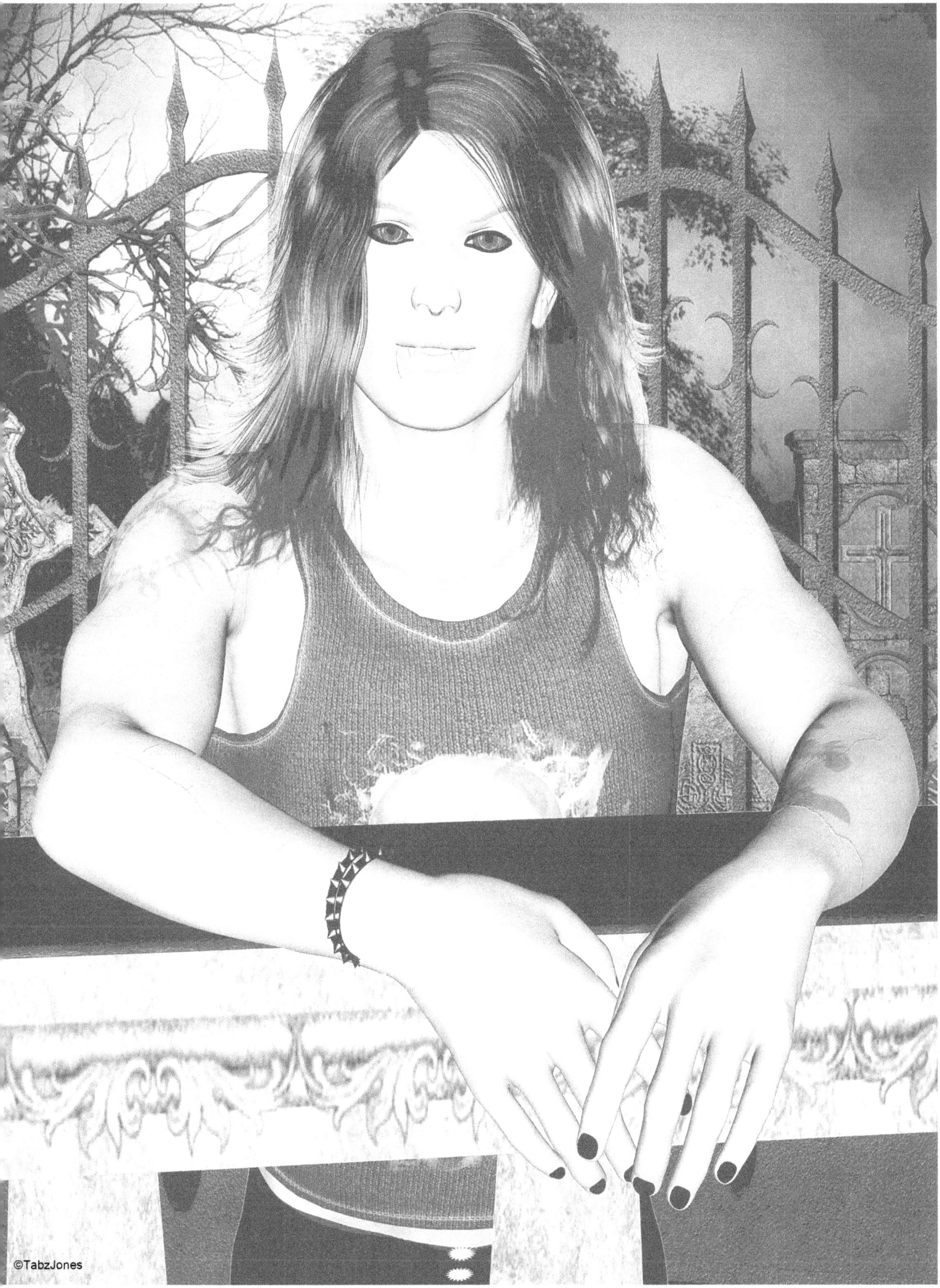

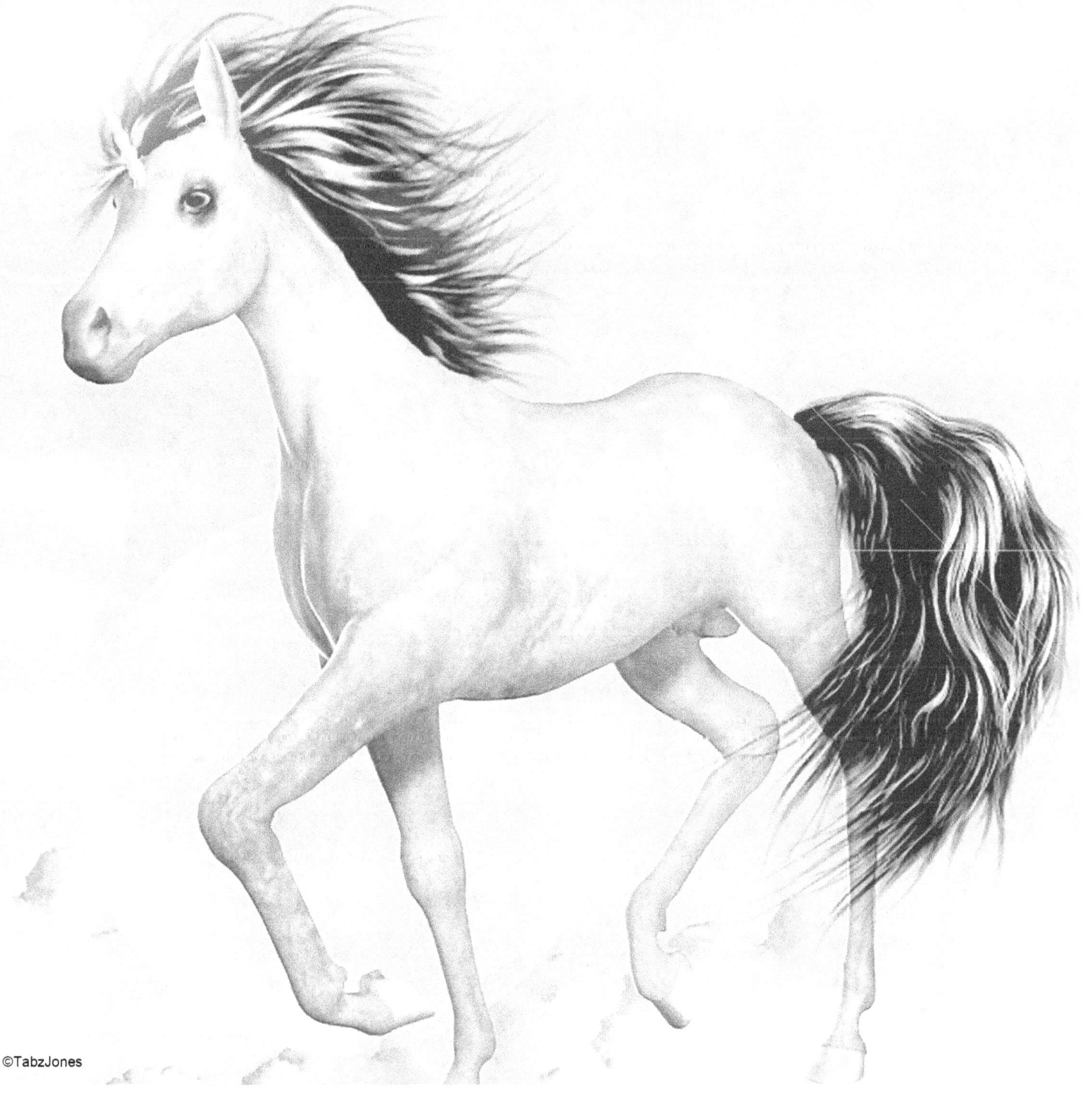

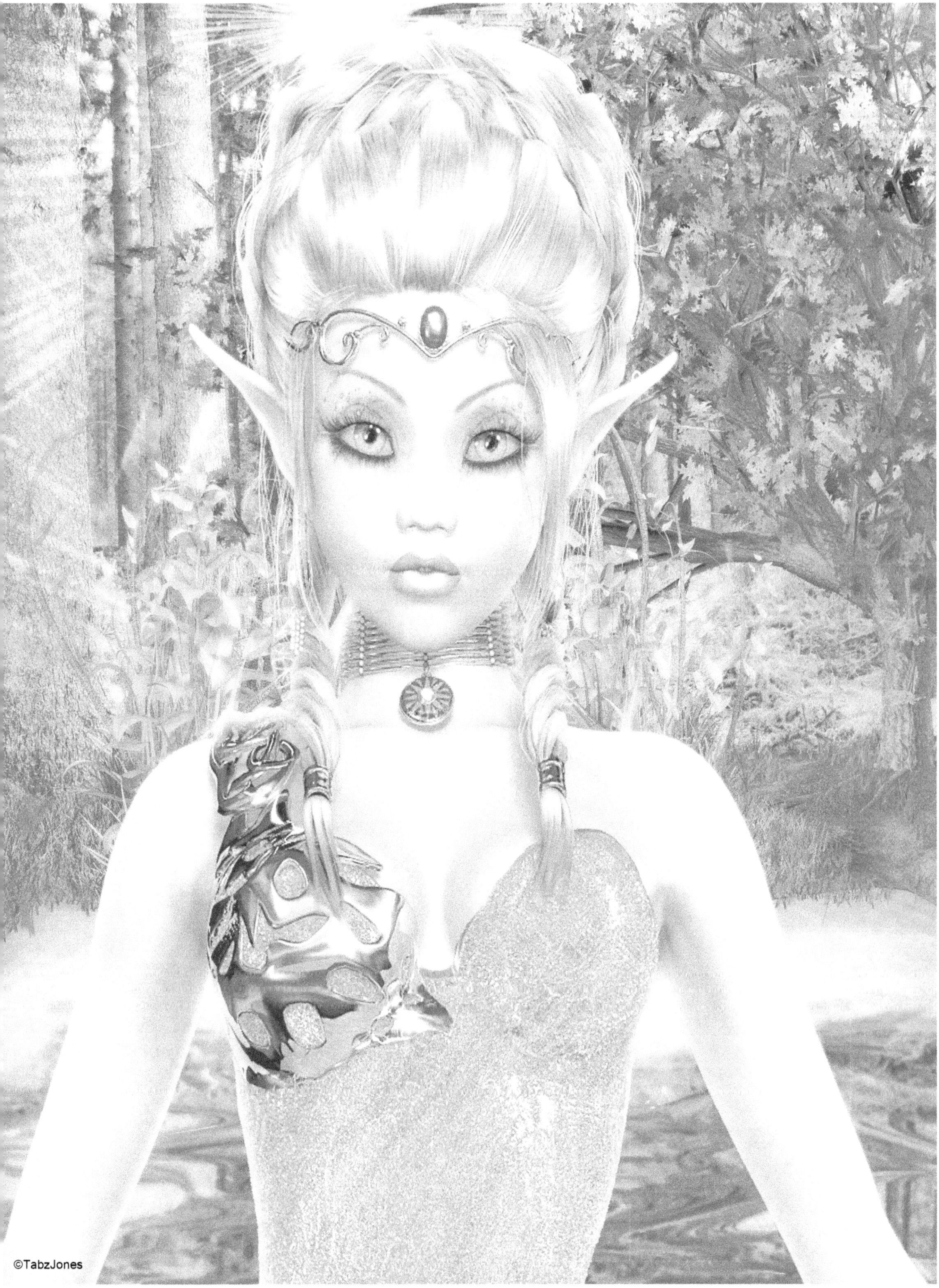

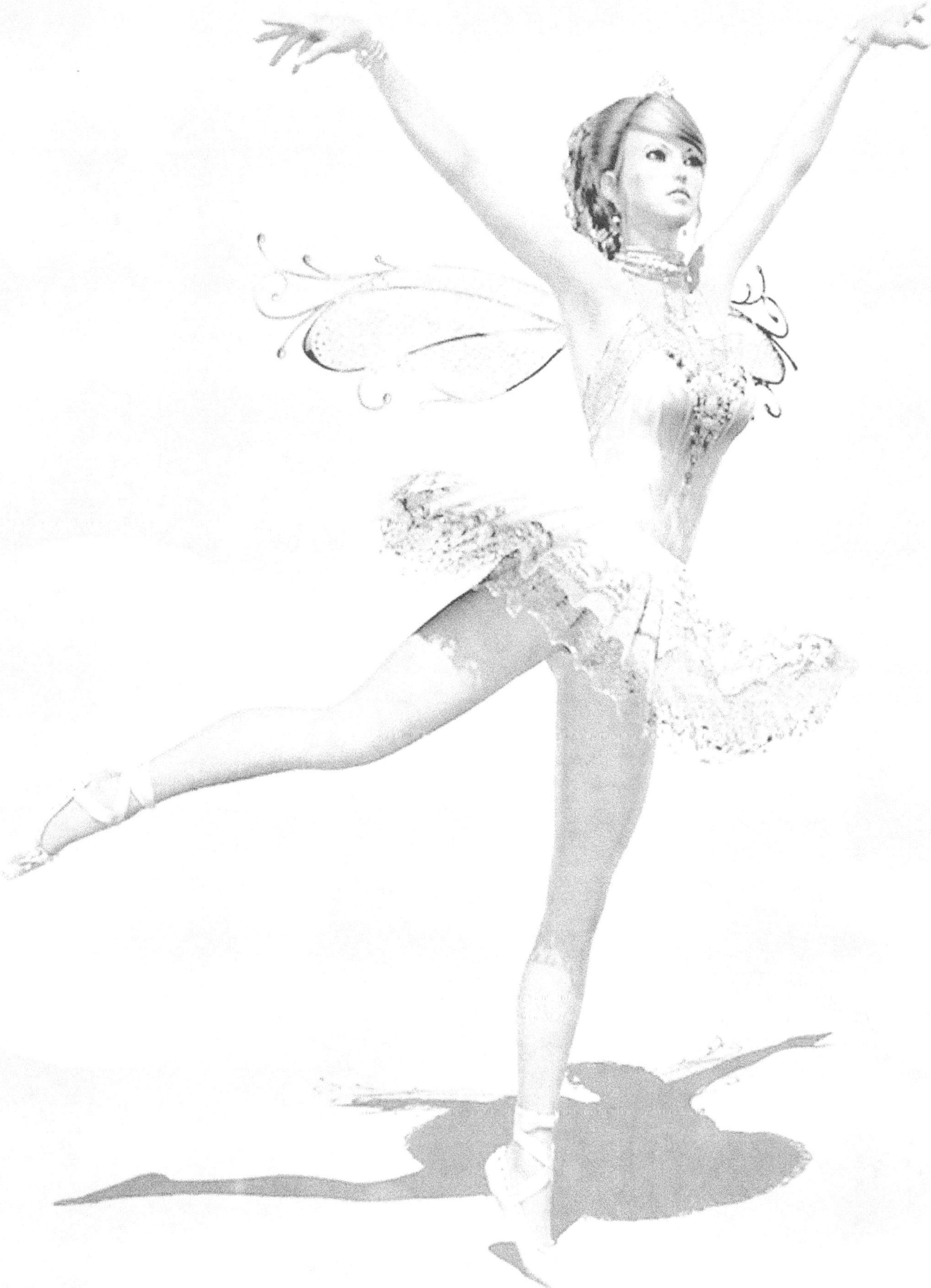

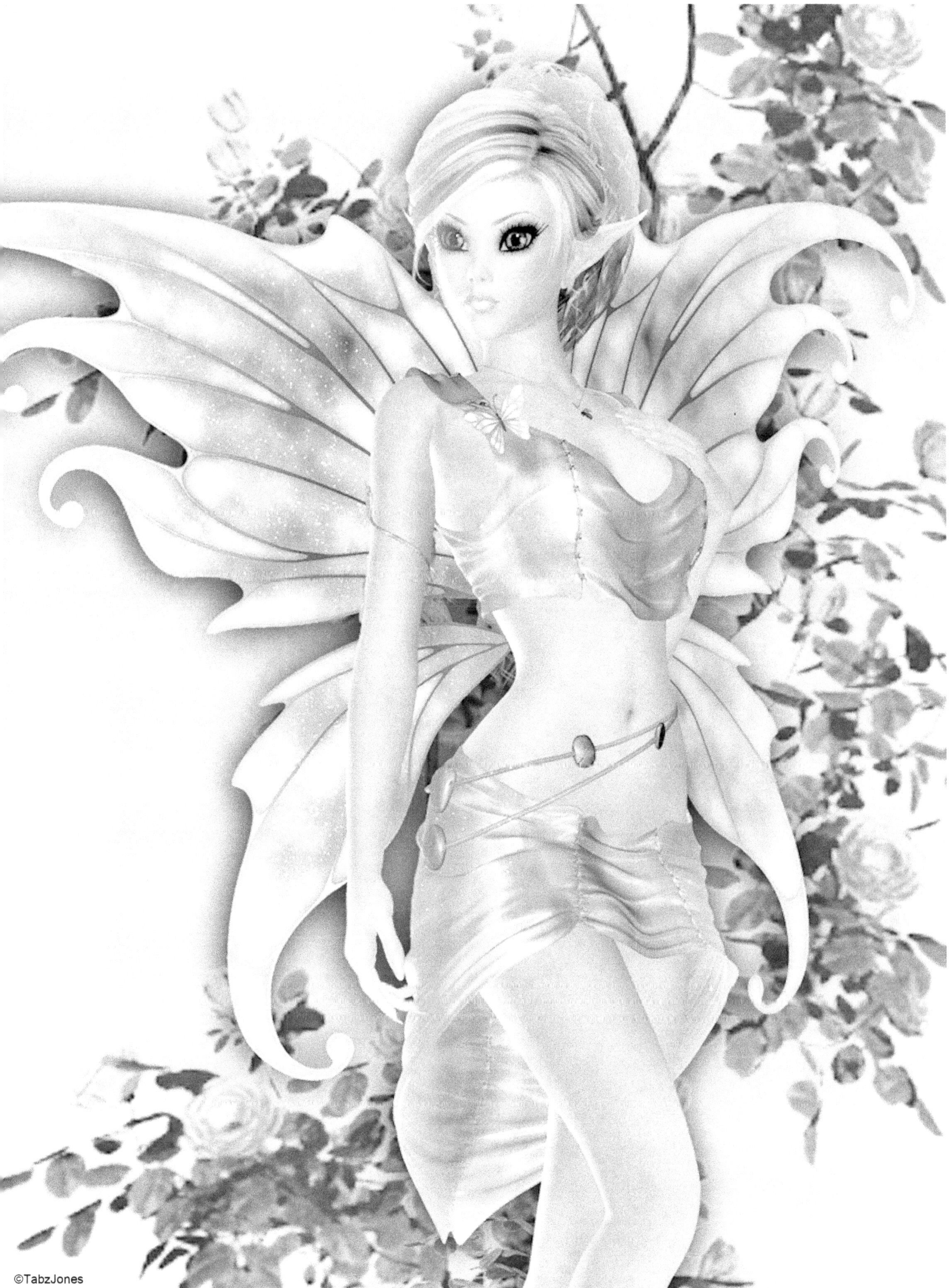

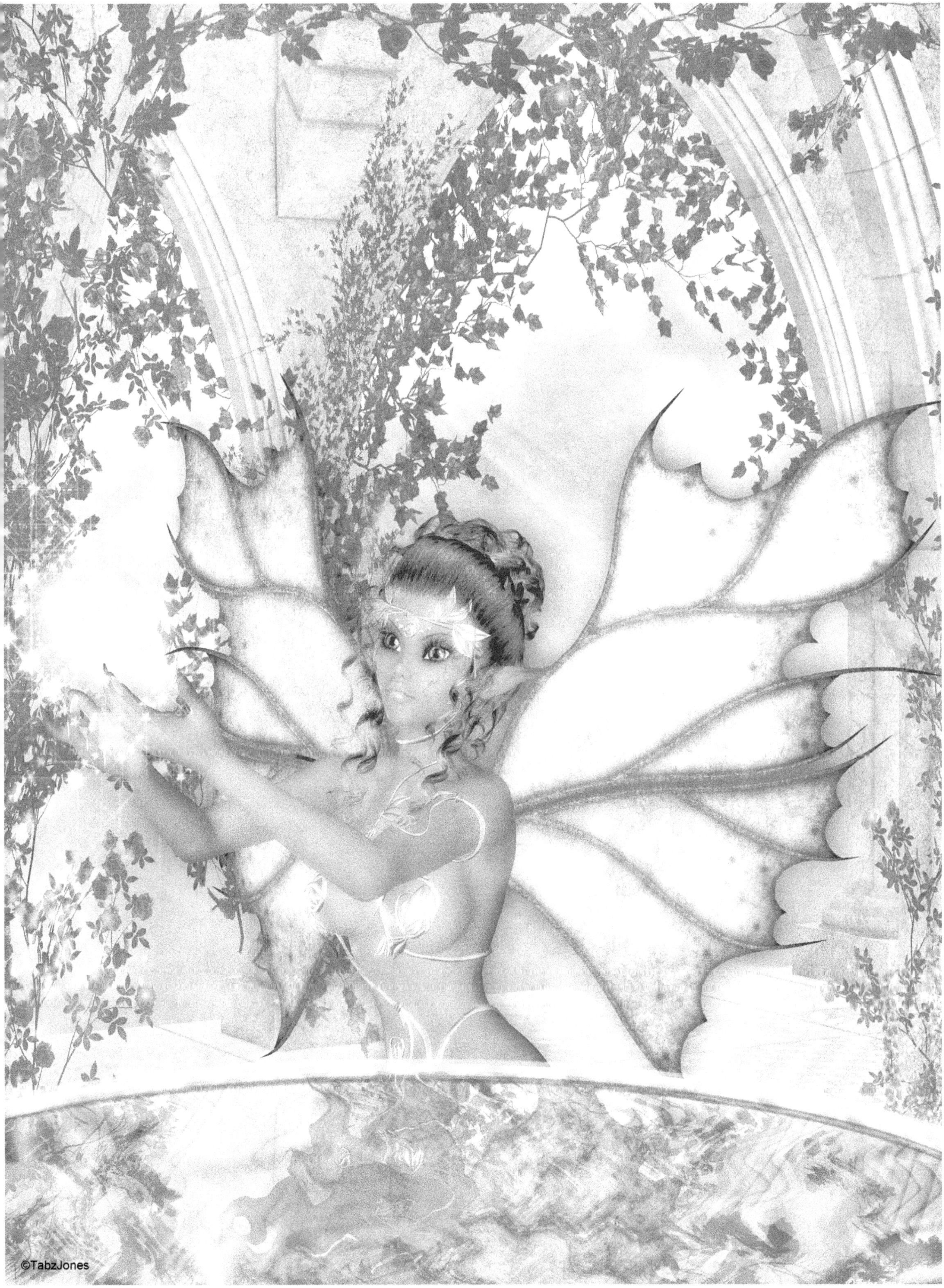
©TabzJones

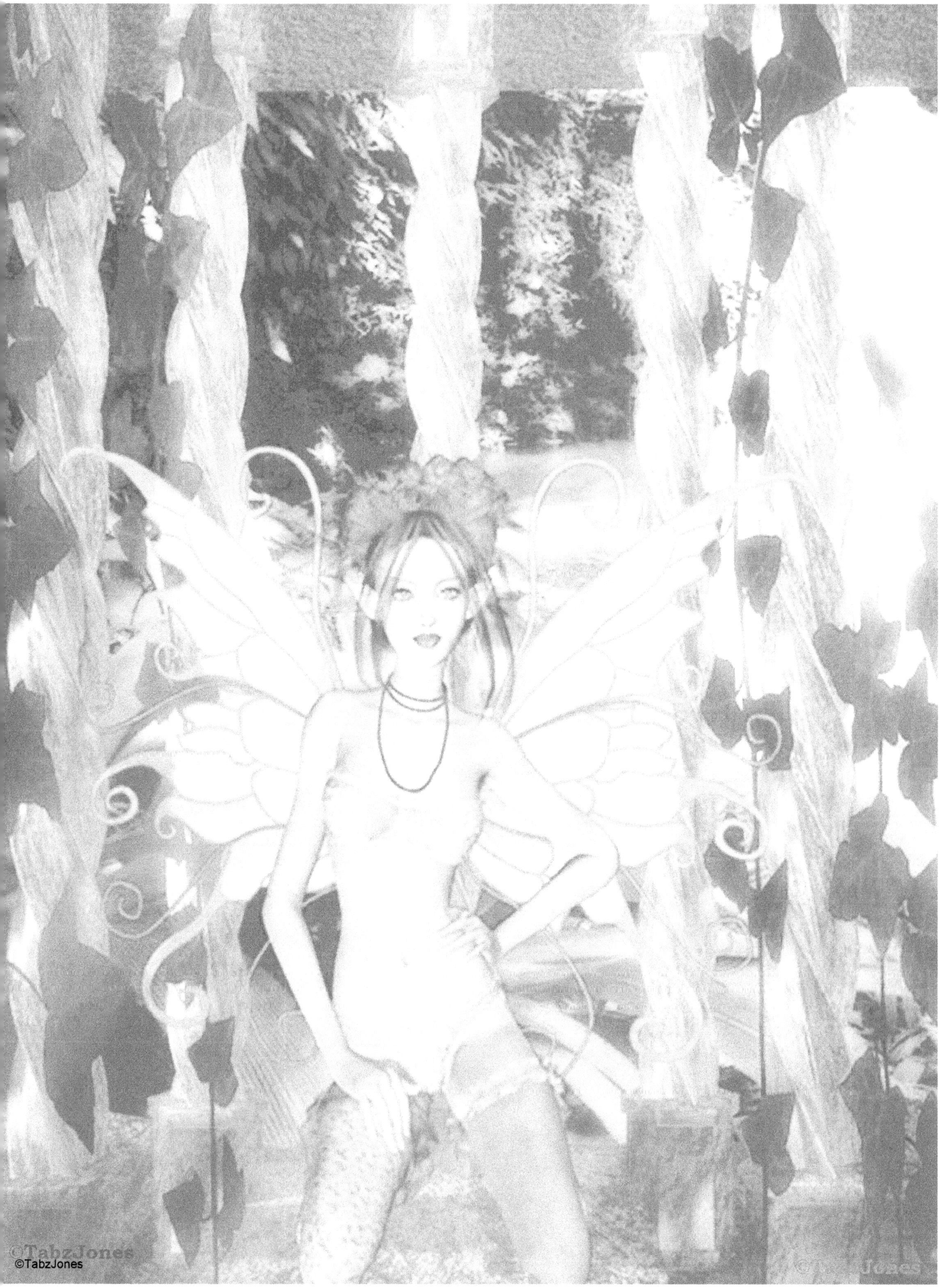
©TabzJones

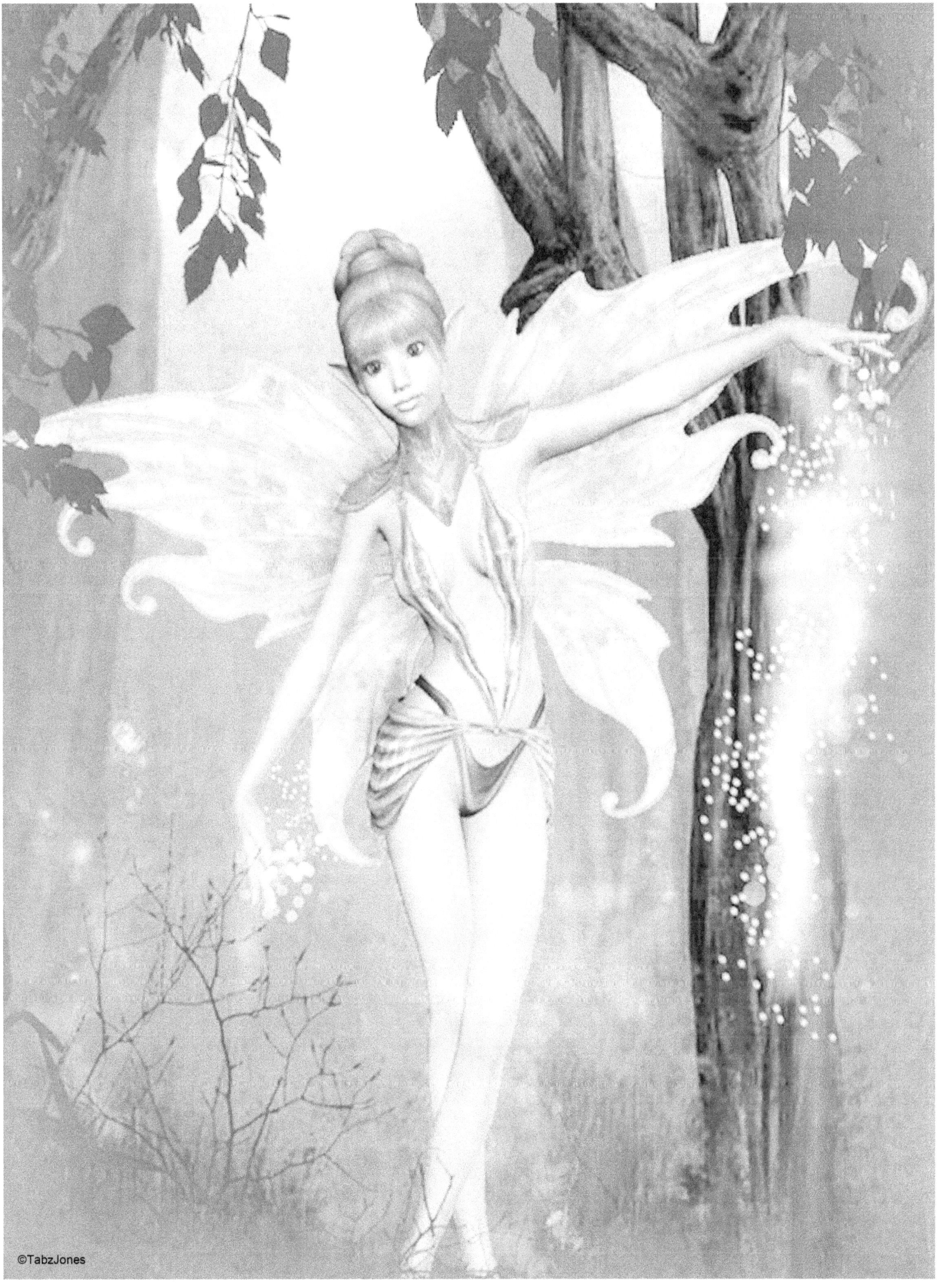

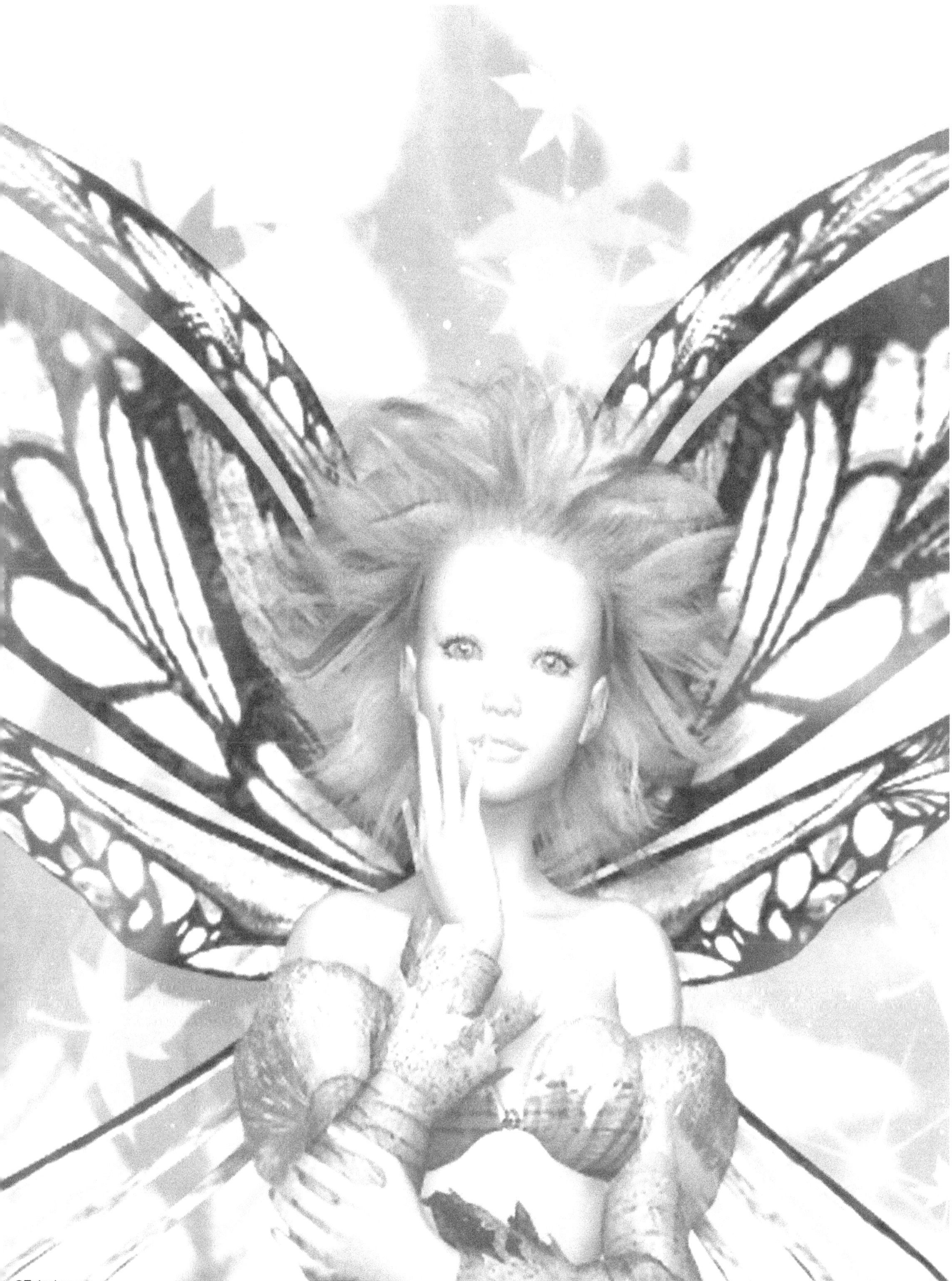

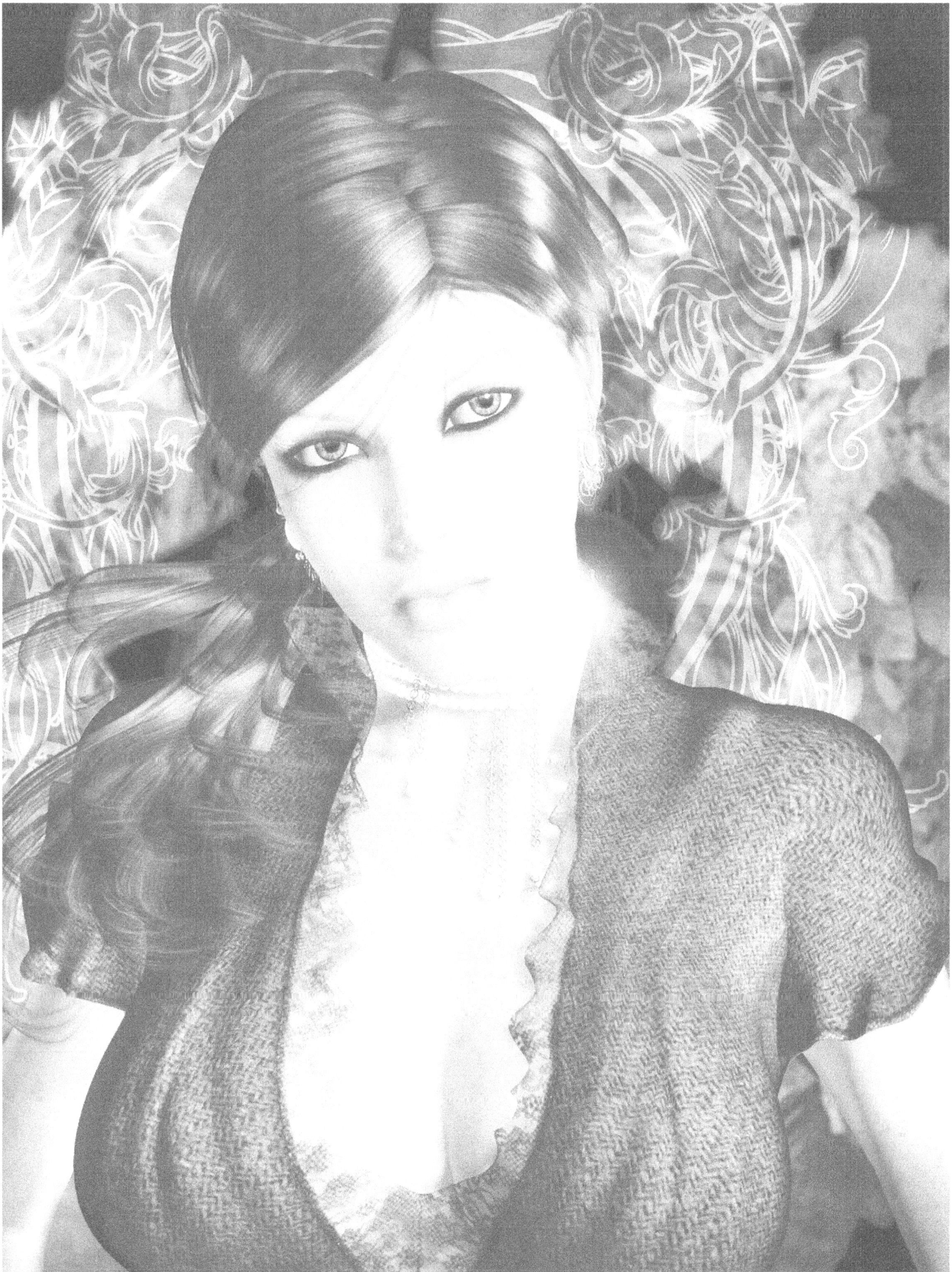

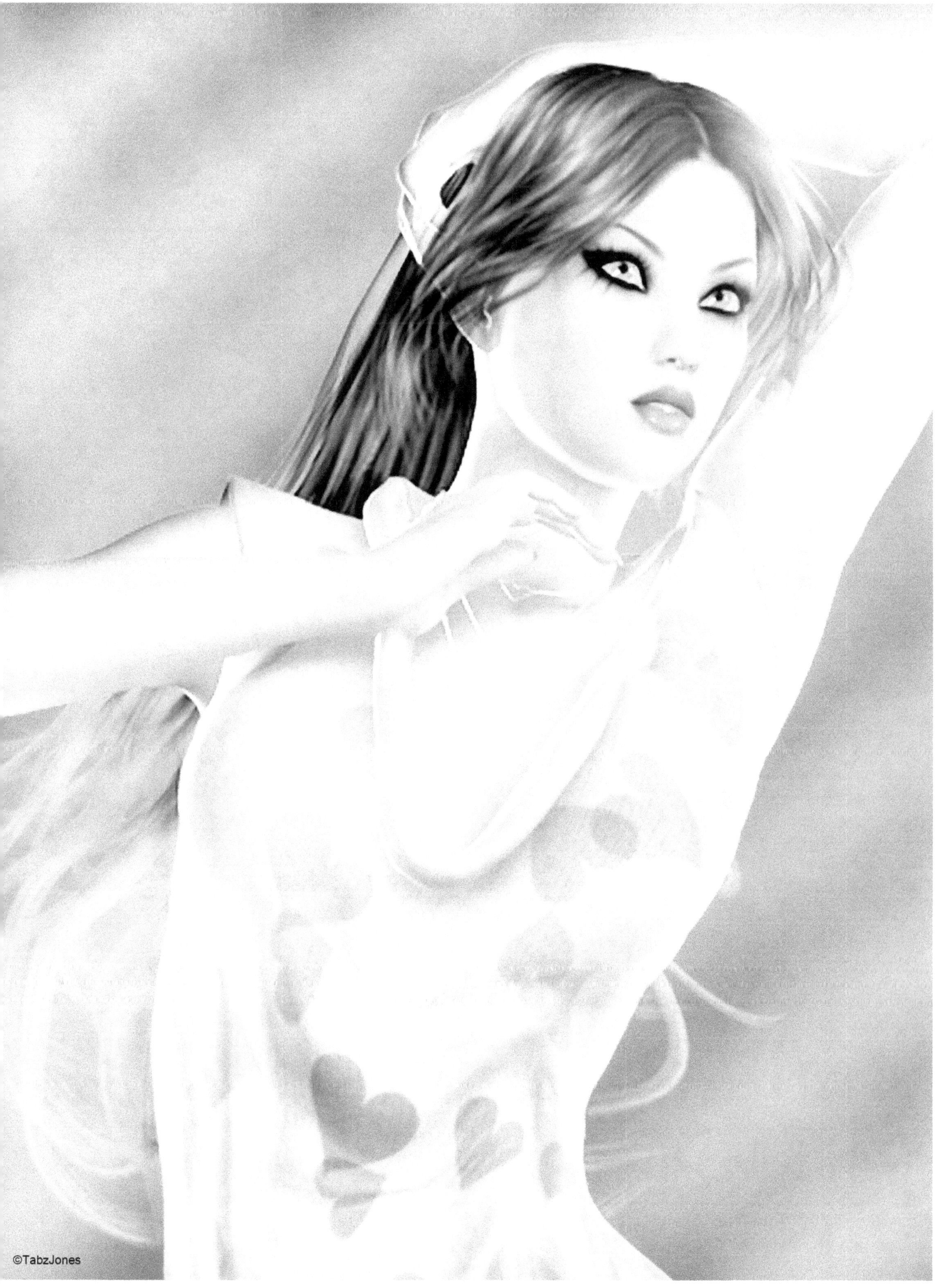

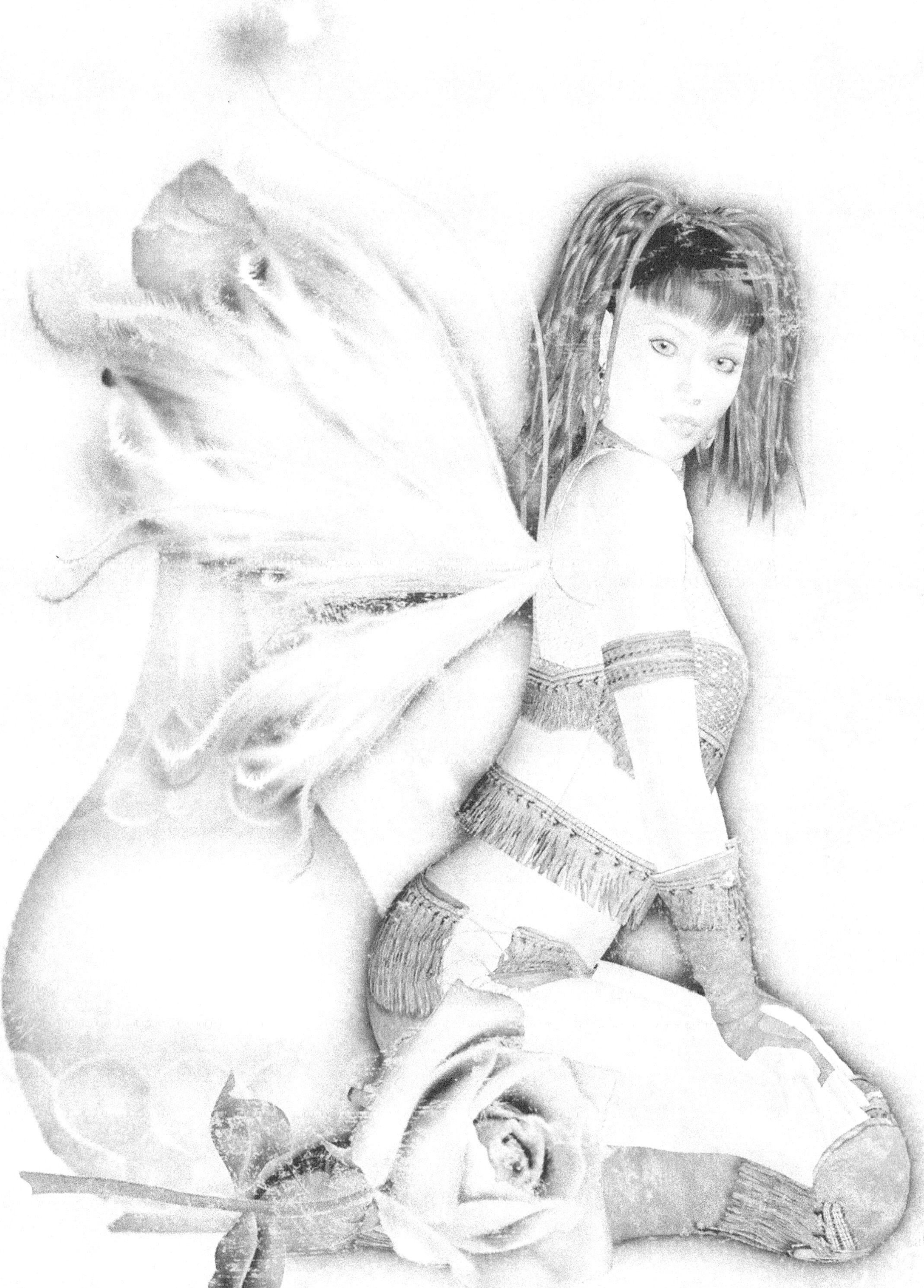

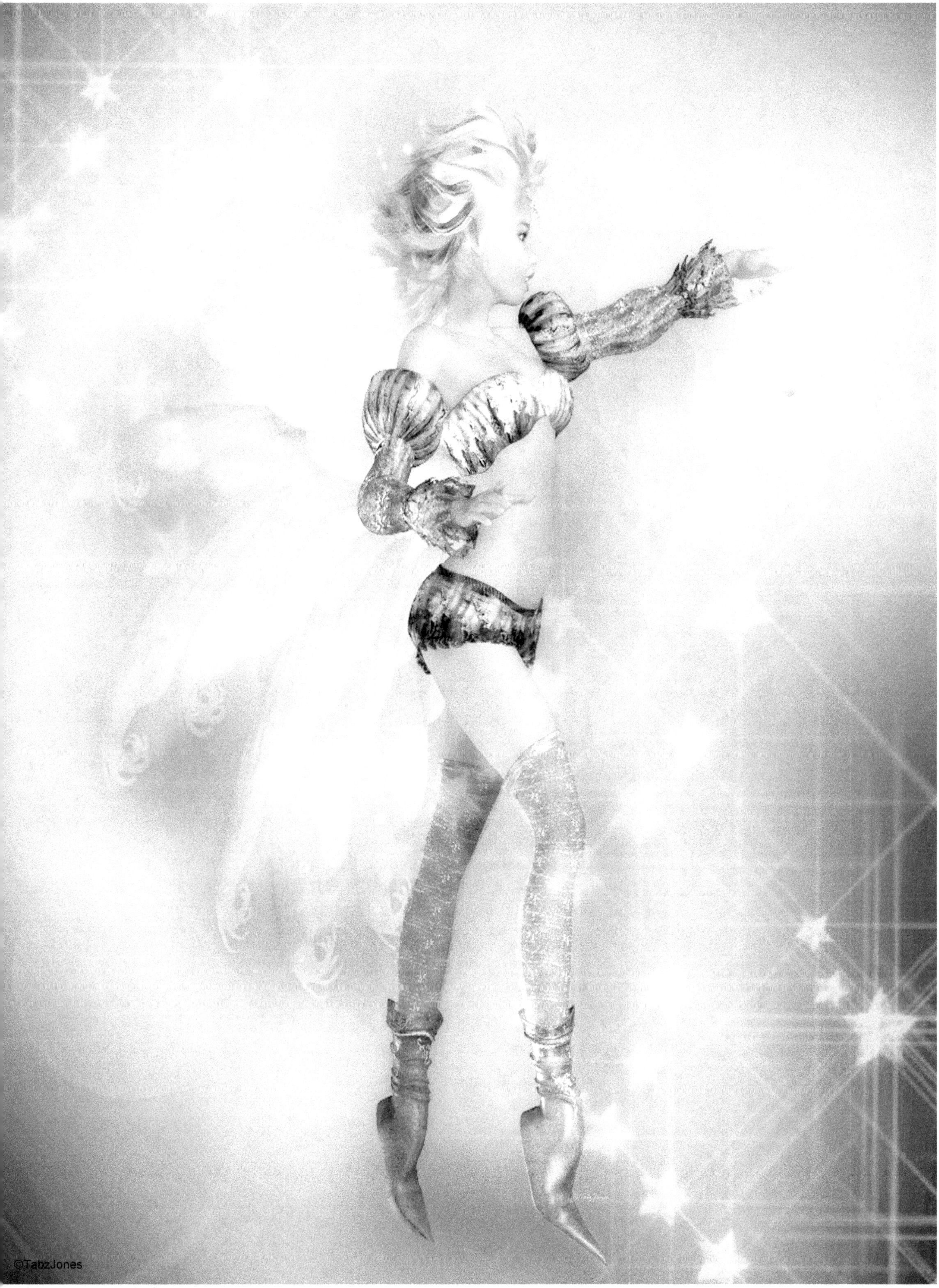
©TabzJones

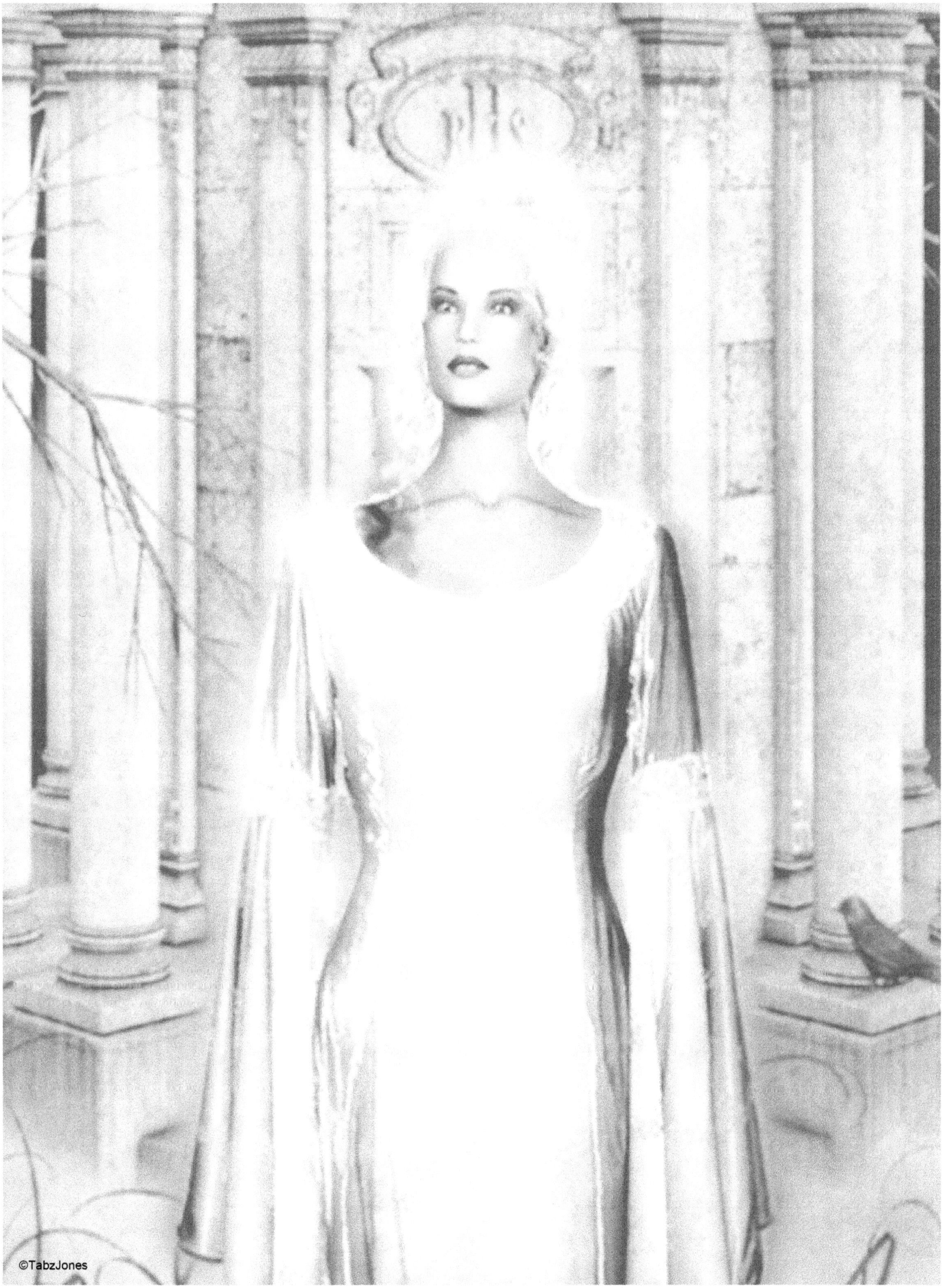
©TabzJones

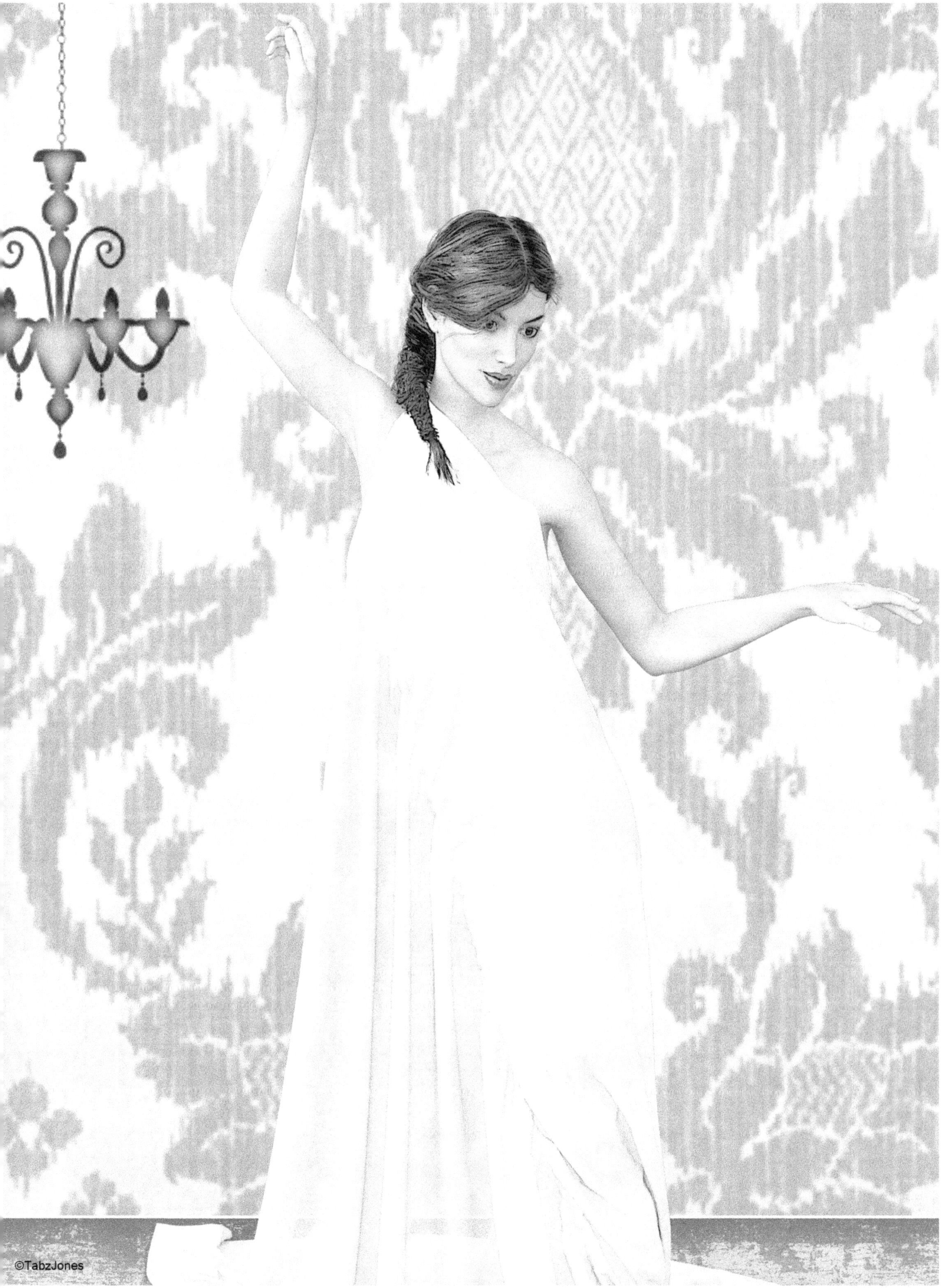
©TabzJones

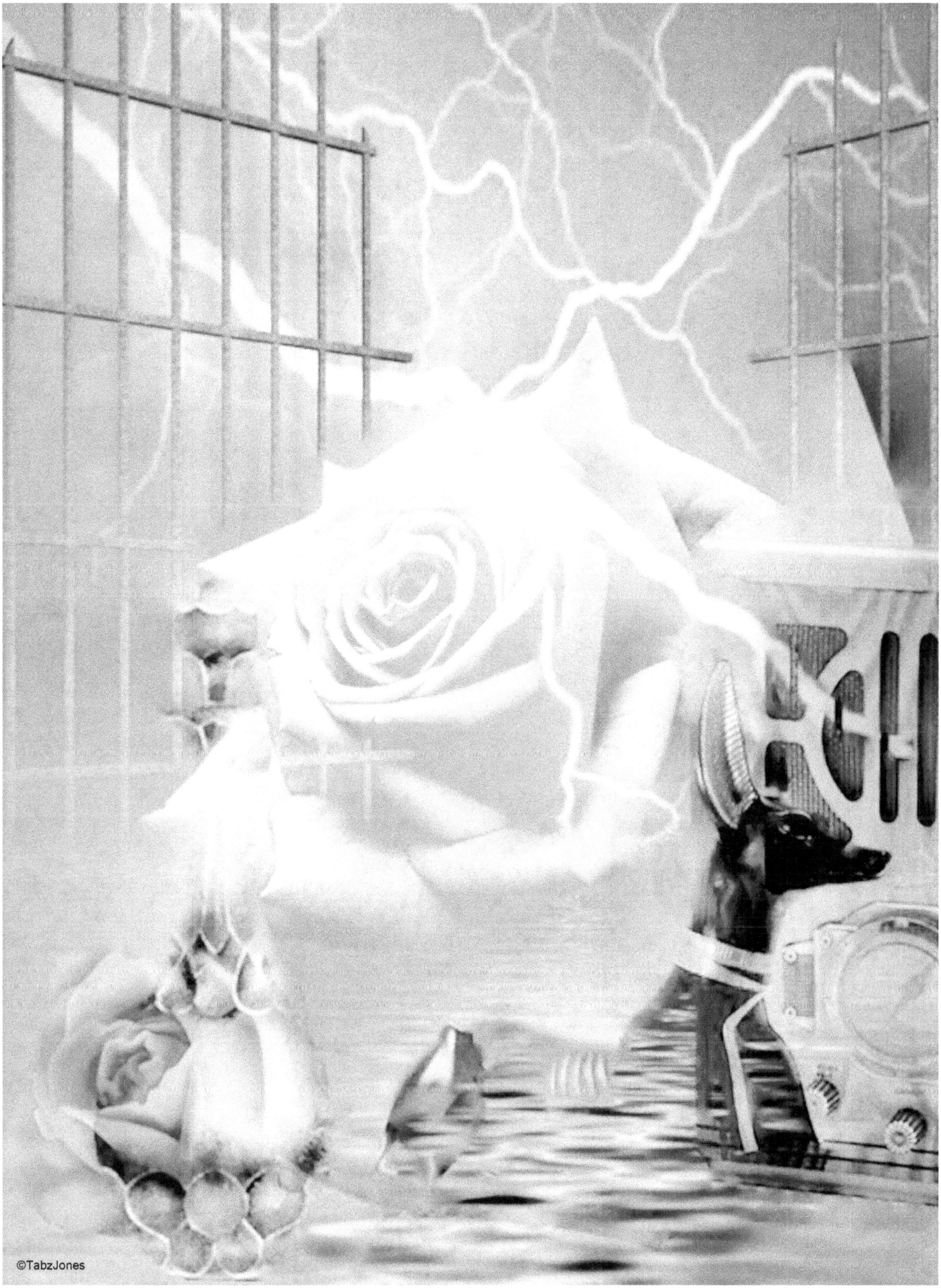
©TabzJones

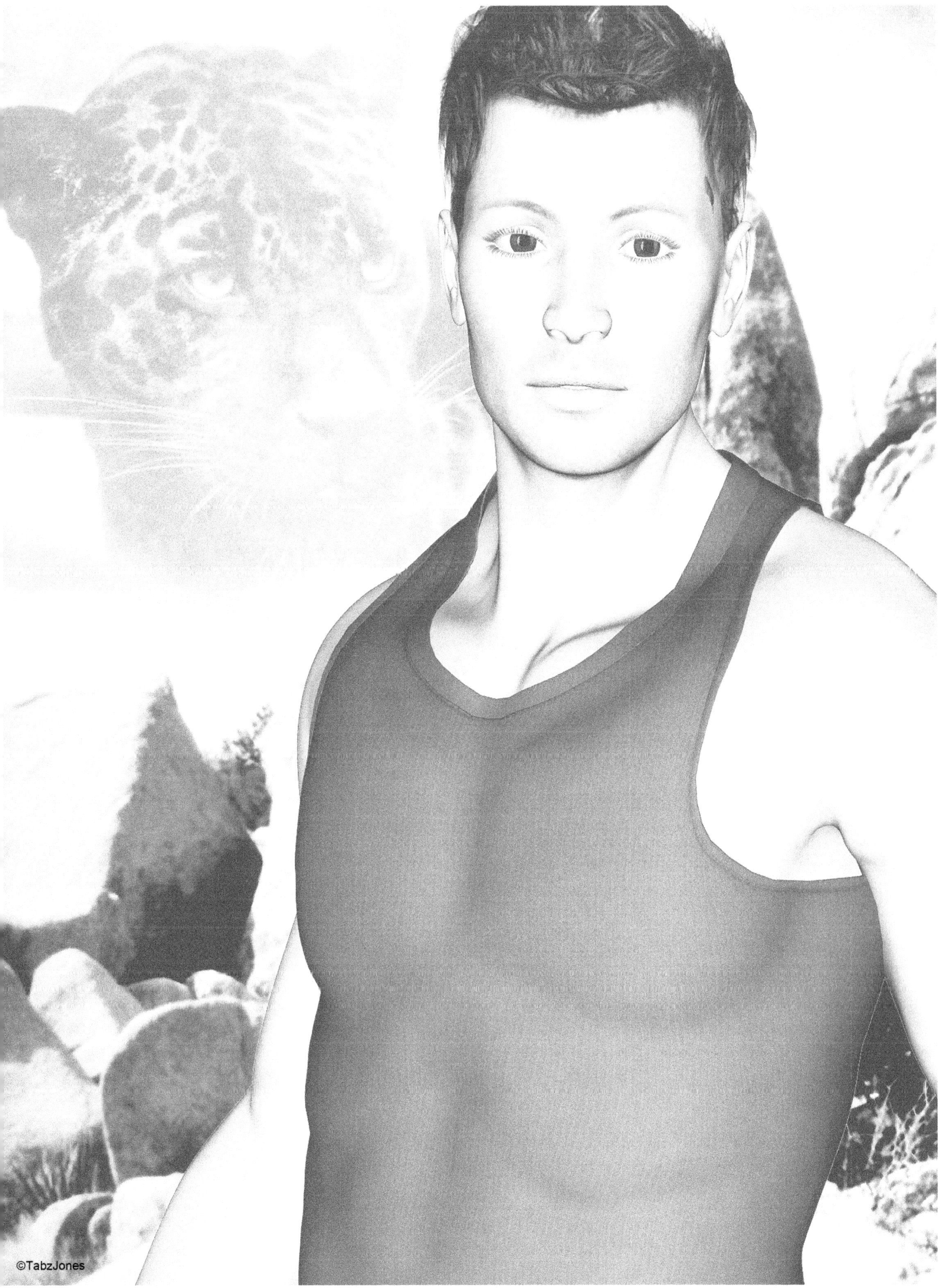

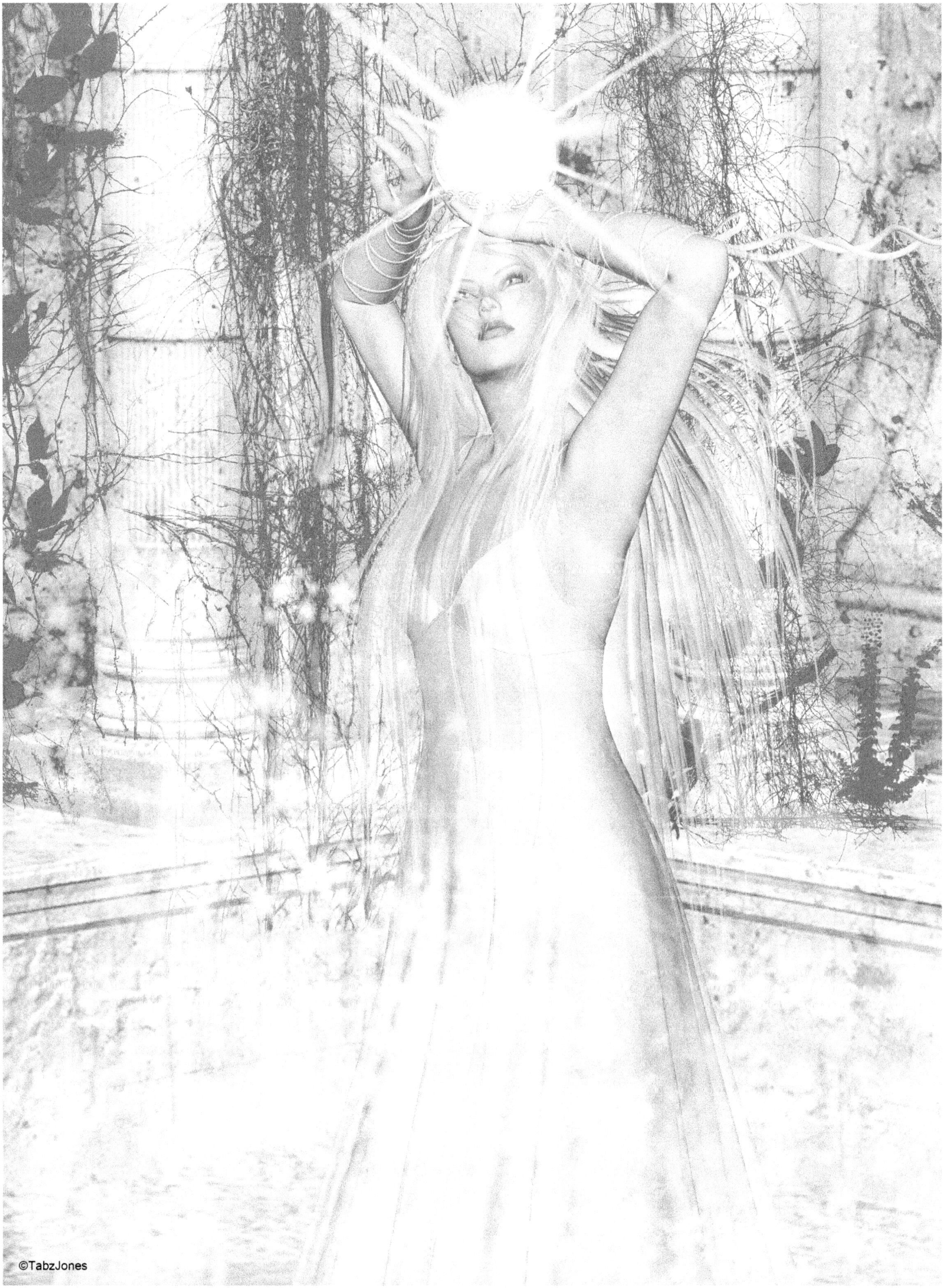

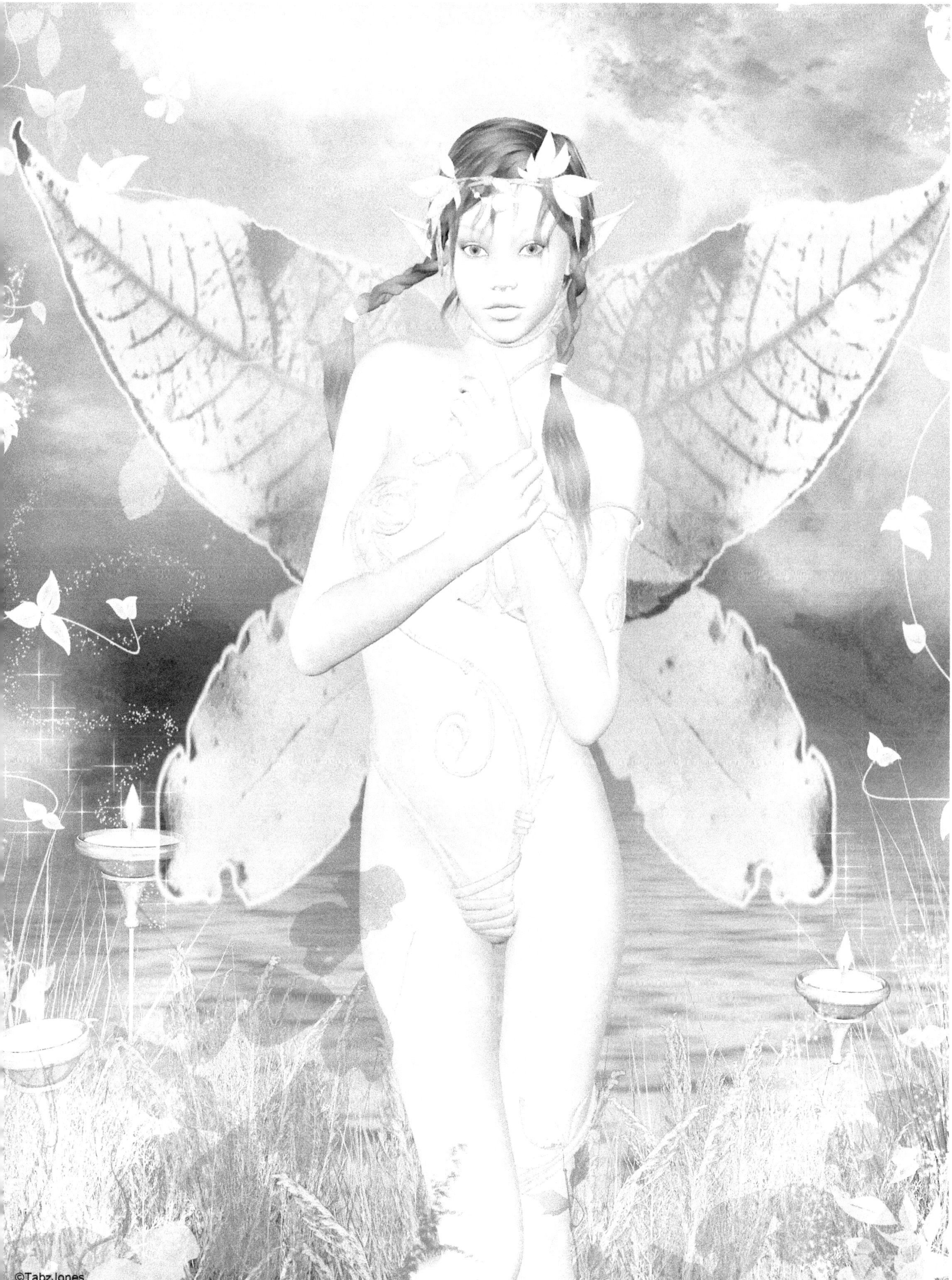
©TabzJones

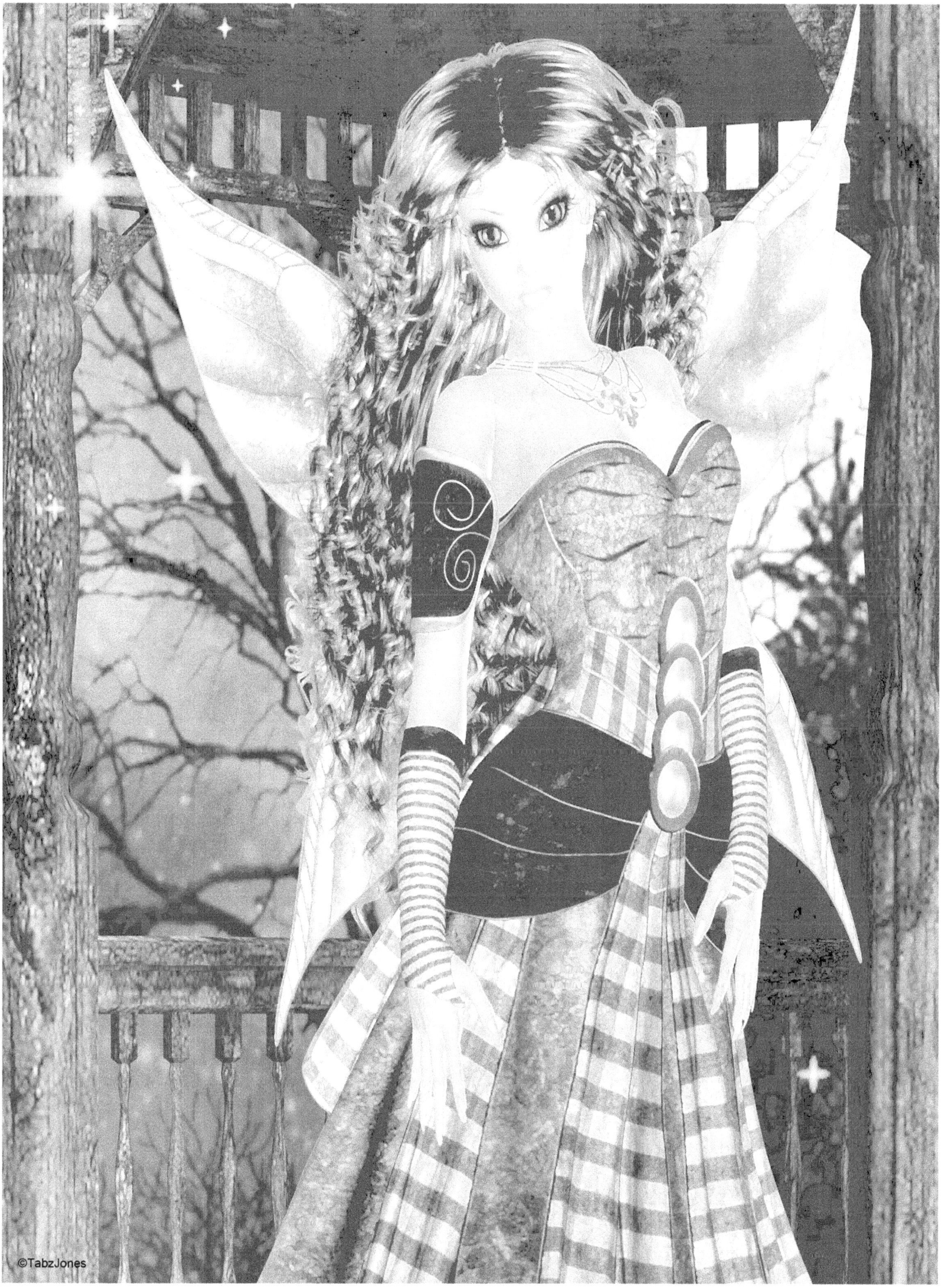

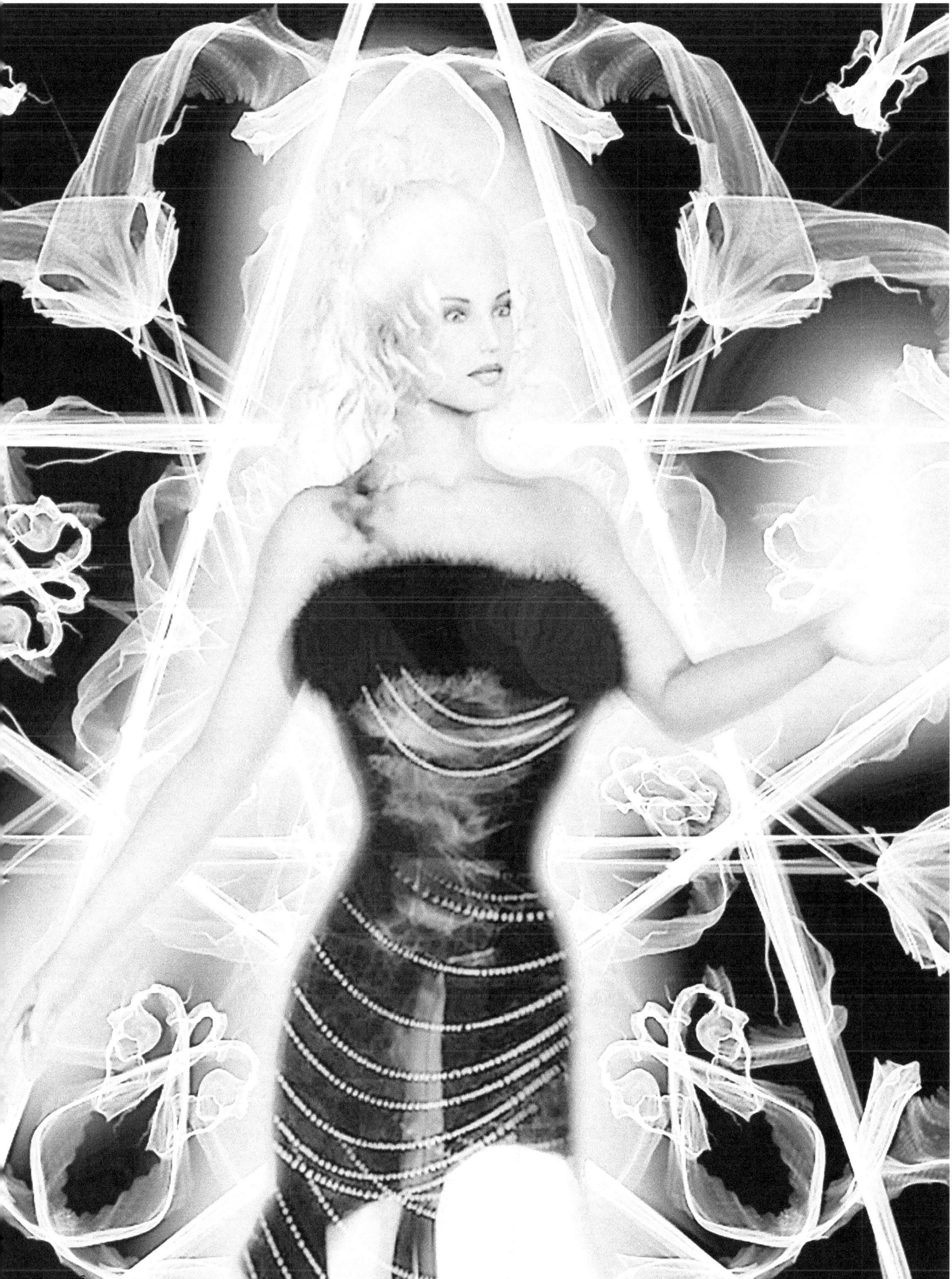

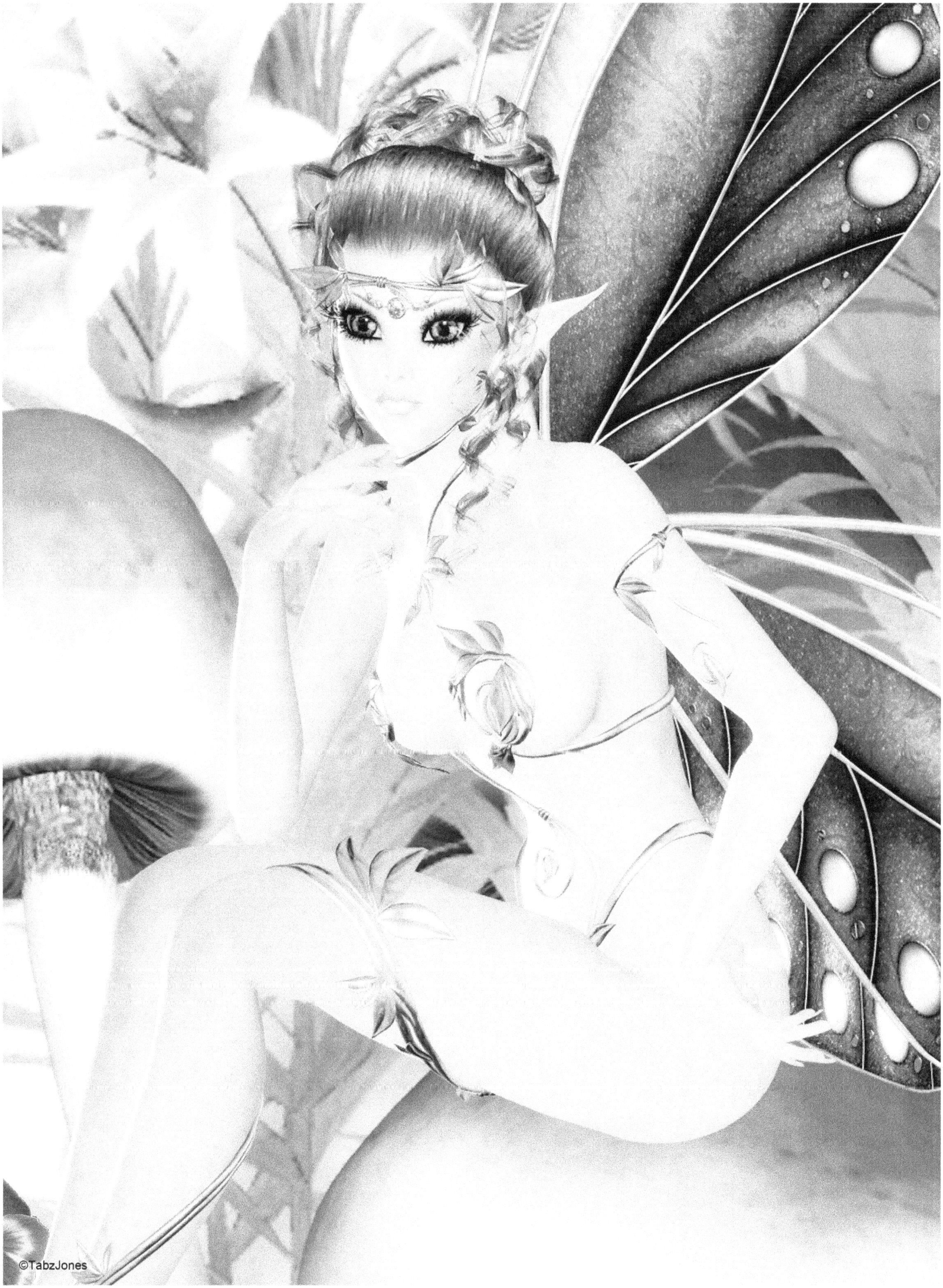

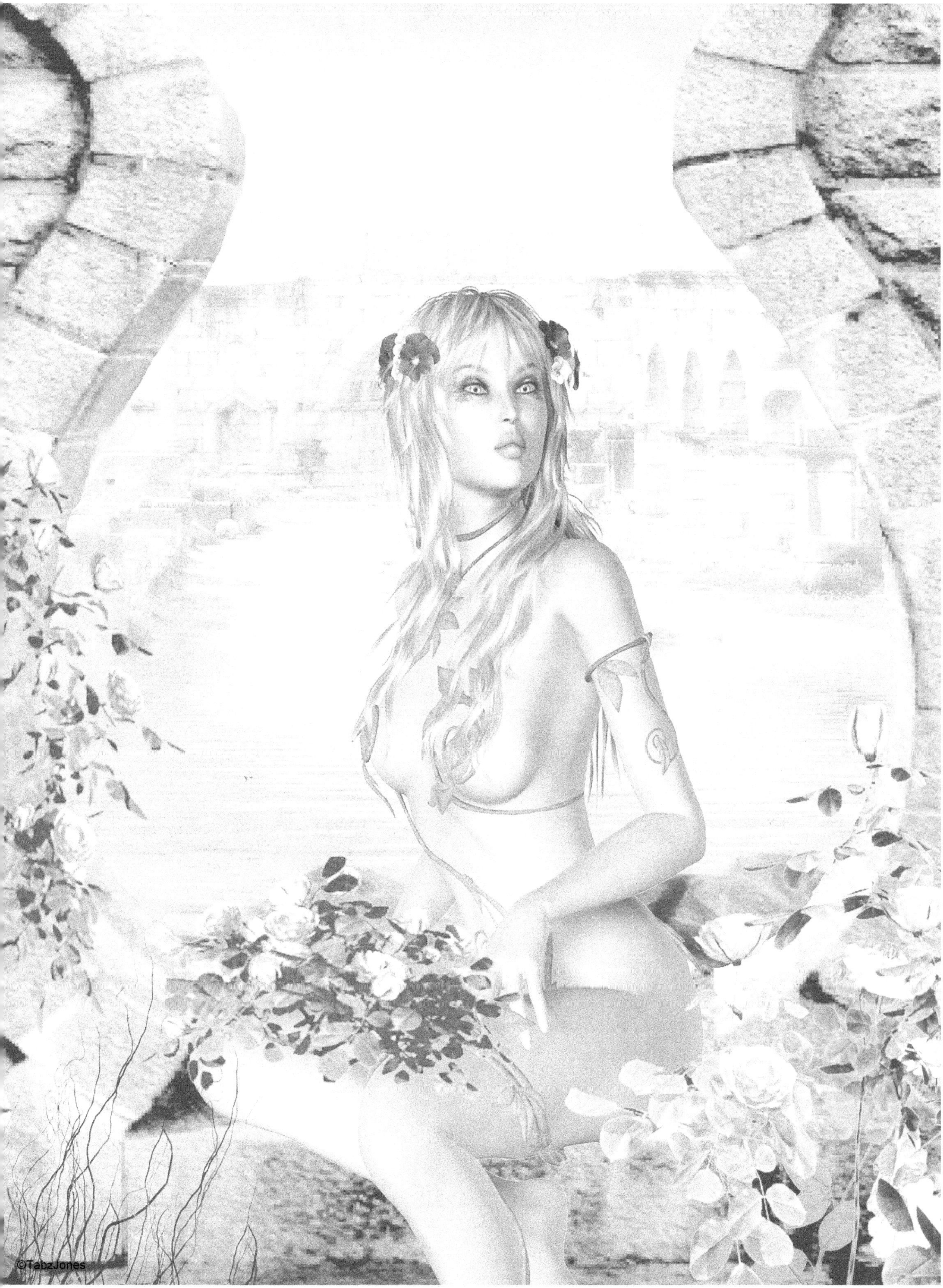
©TabzJones

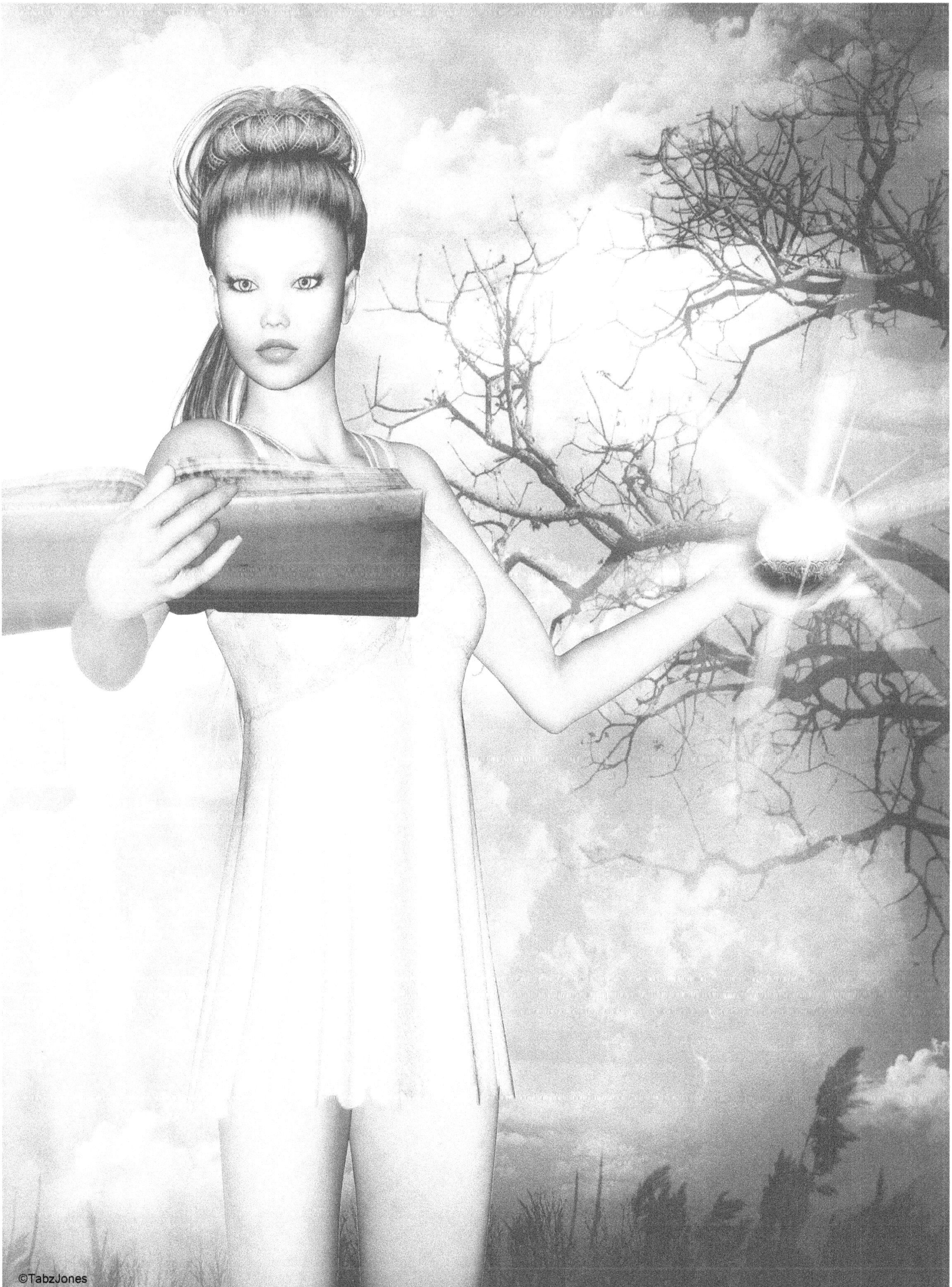
©TabzJones

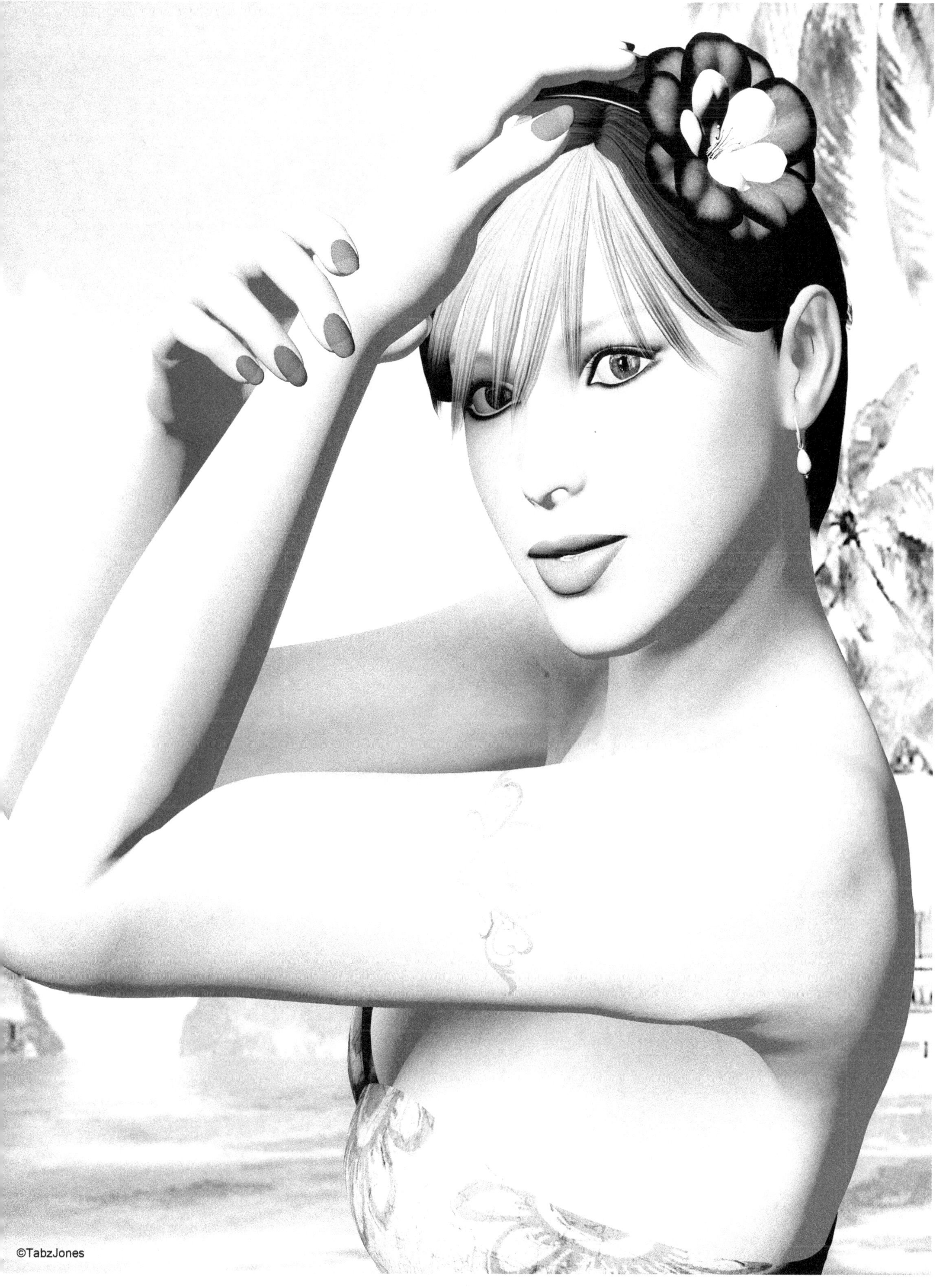

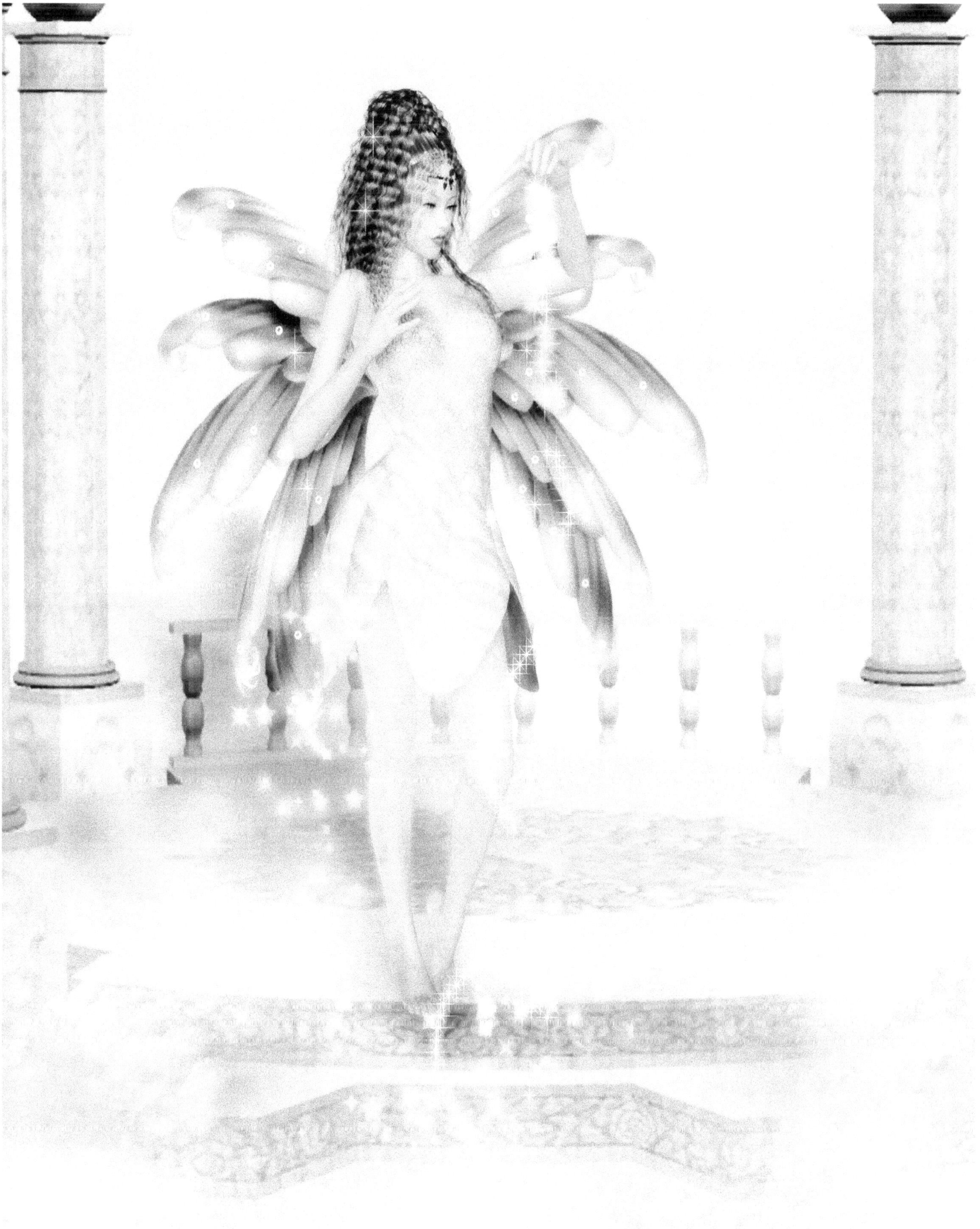

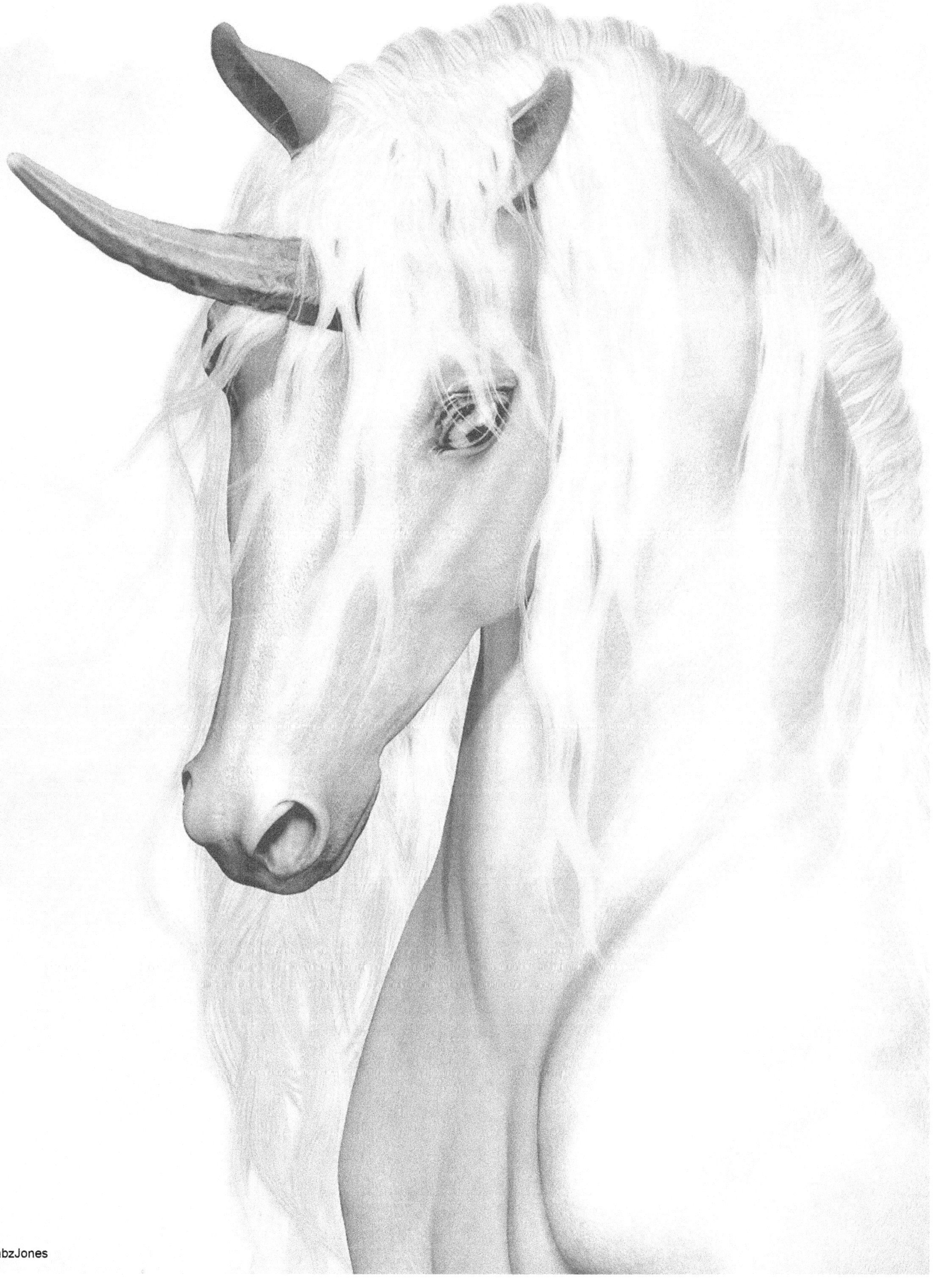

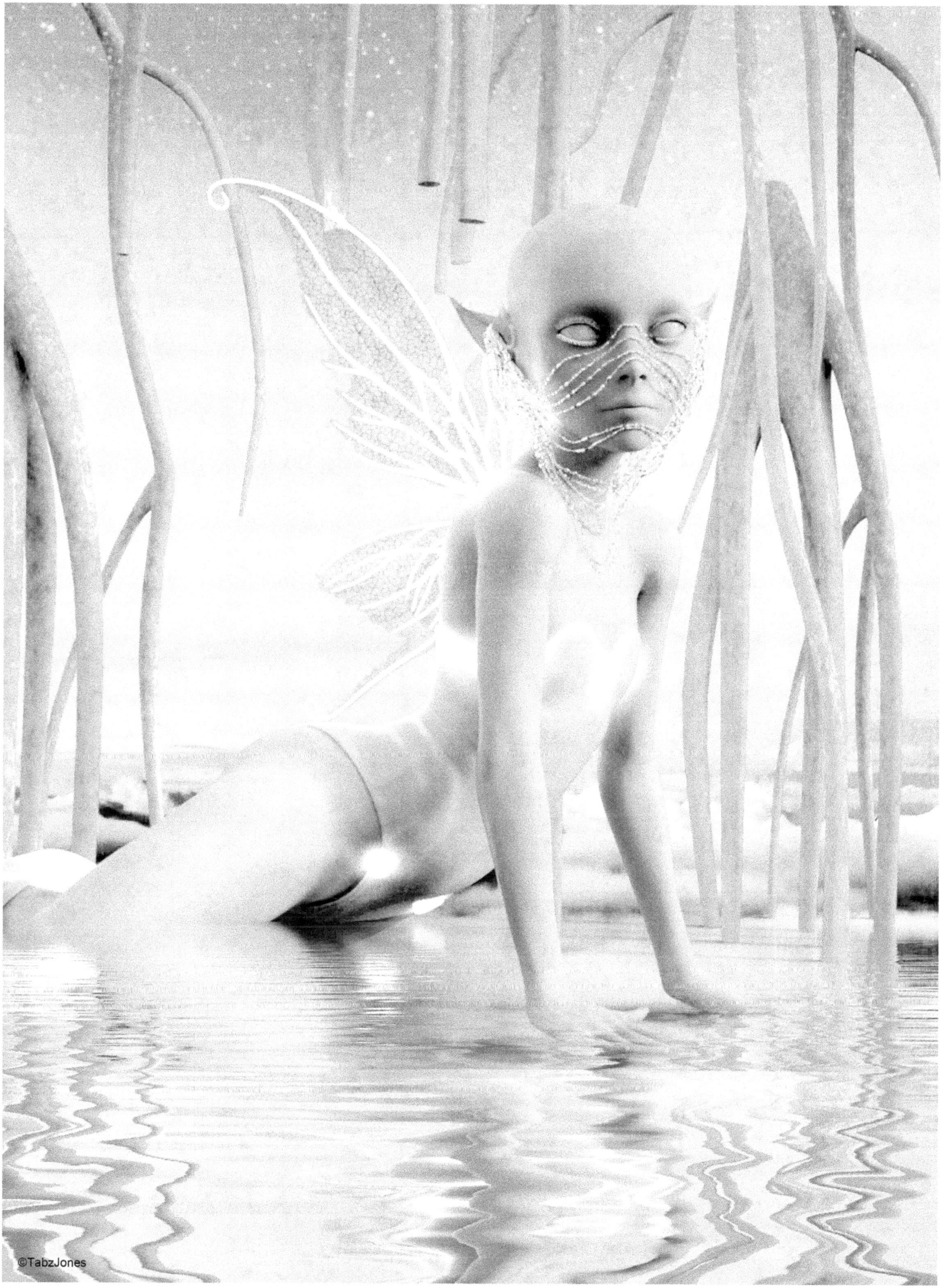
©TabzJones

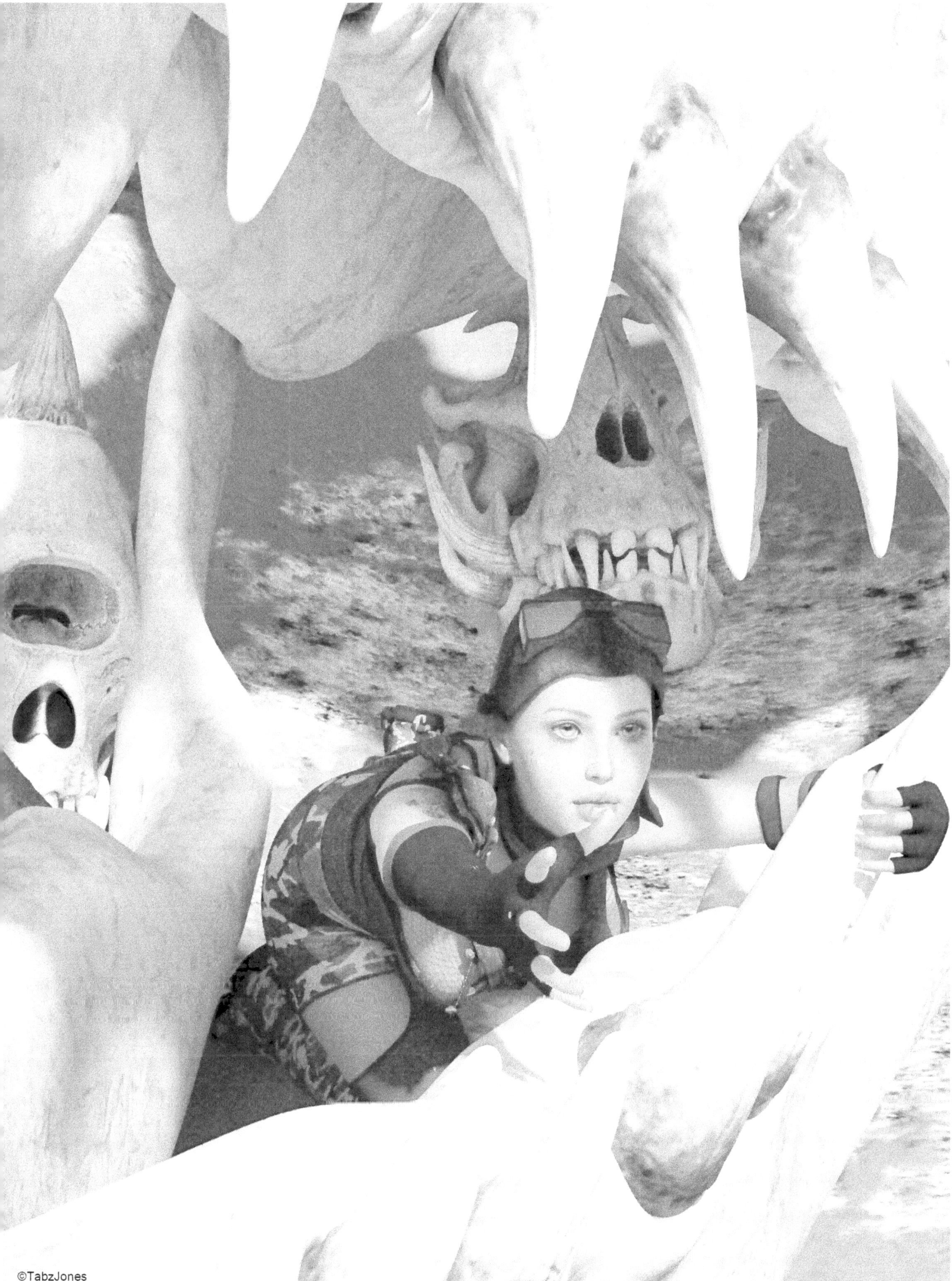

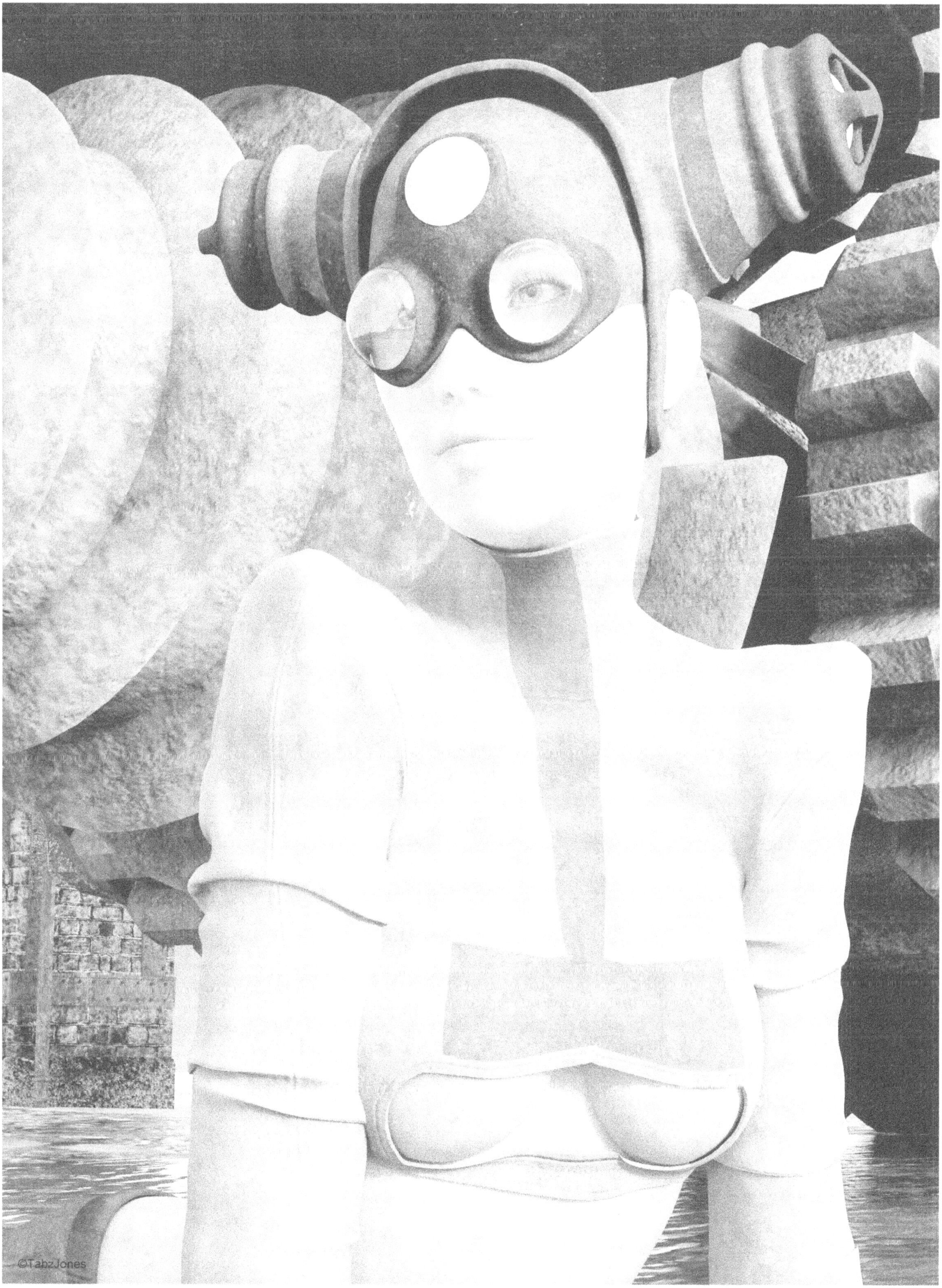

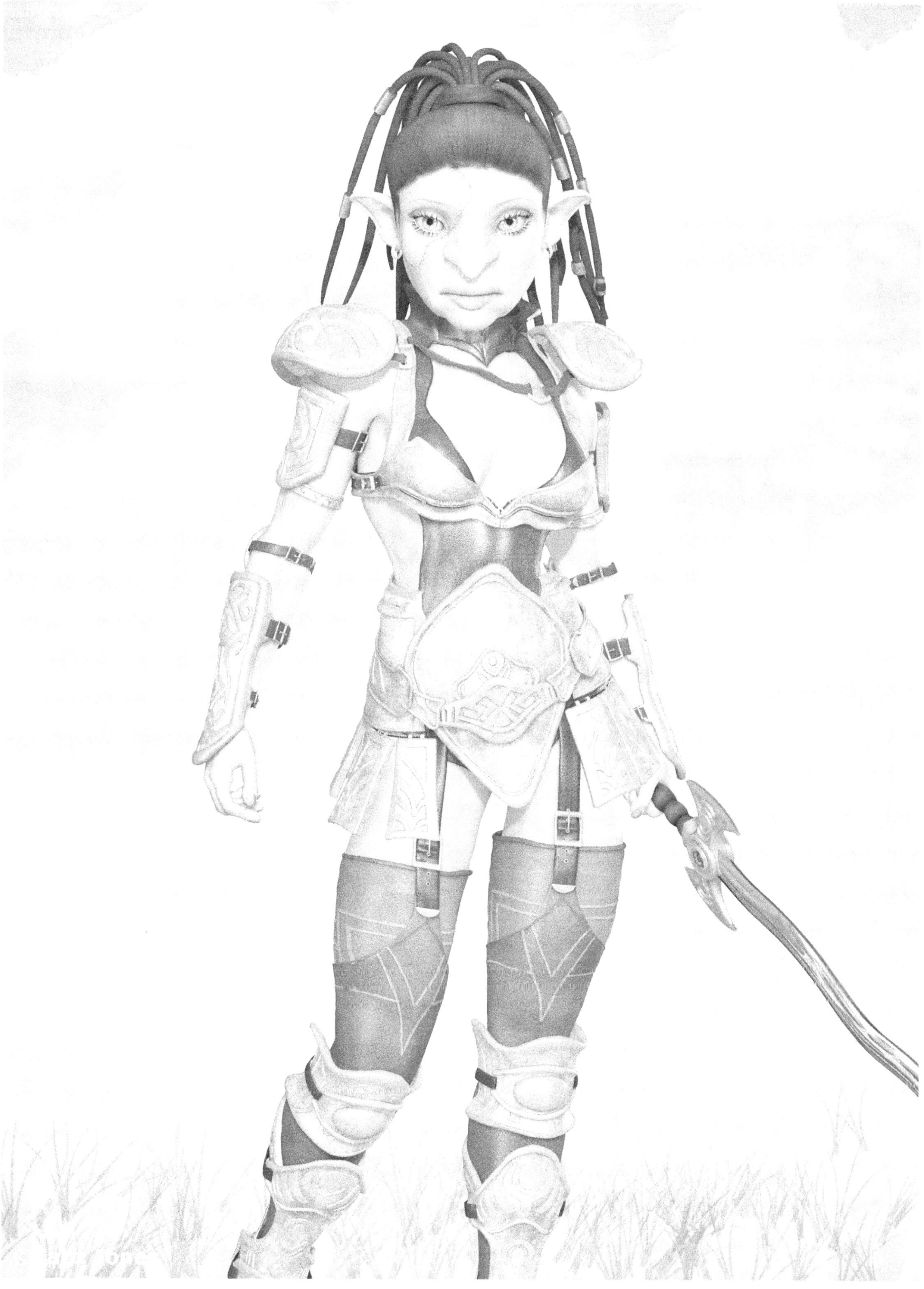

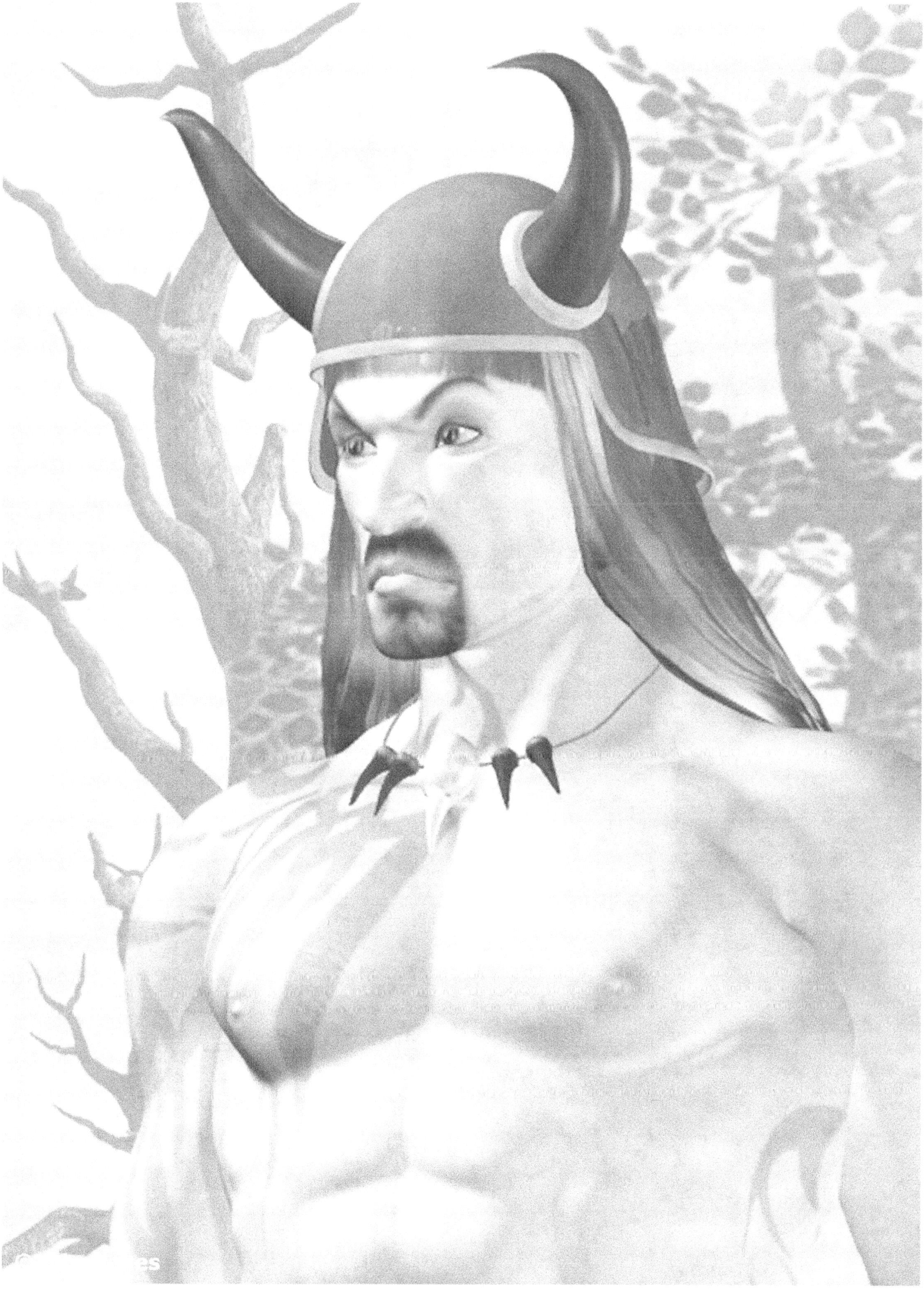

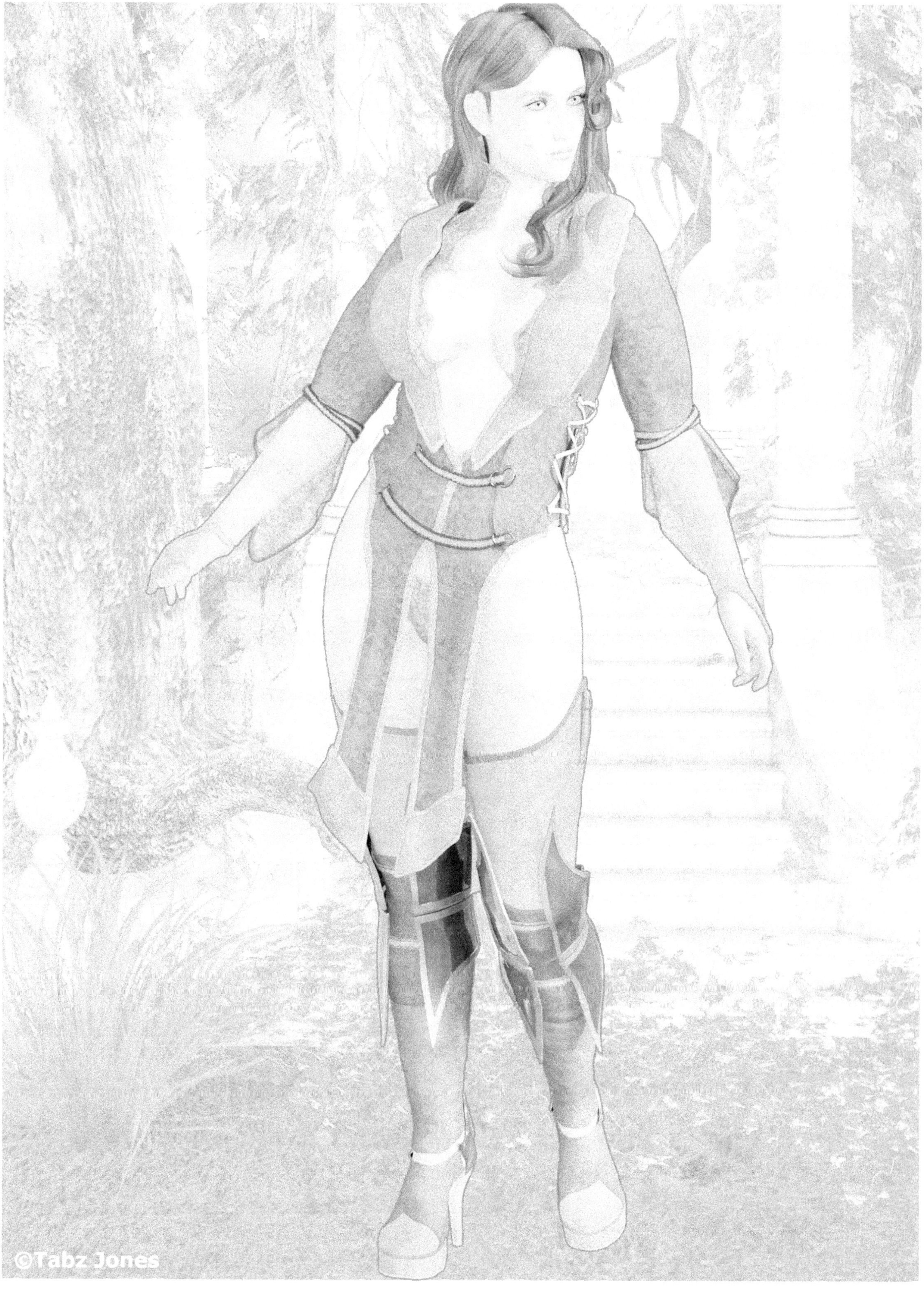
©Tabz Jones

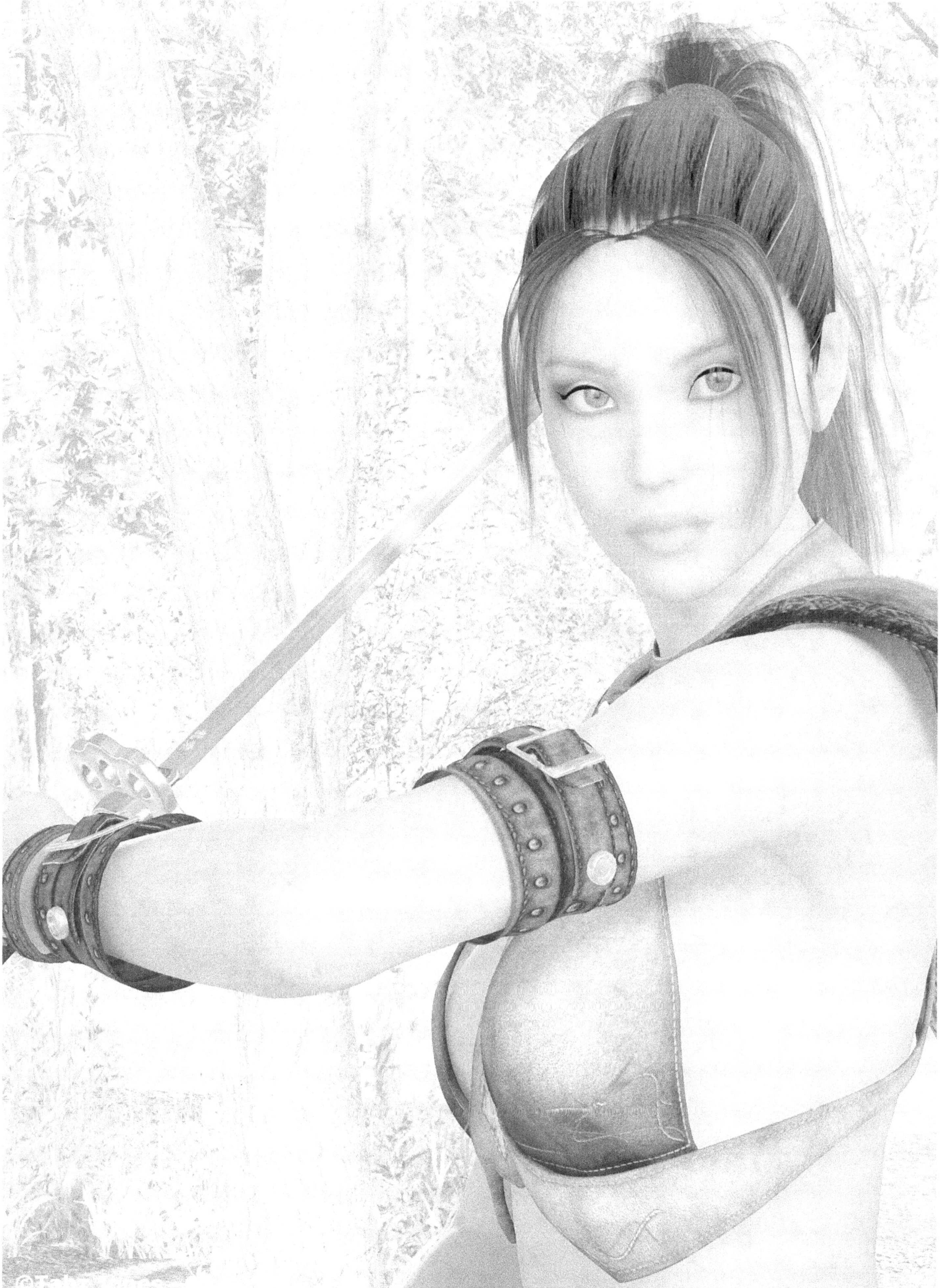

www.ingramcontent.com/pod-product-compliance
Lightning Source LLC
Chambersburg PA
CBHW081733220526
45468CB00008B/2082